Never the Same

A Fresh Look at the Sermon on the Mount
Matthew 5–7

Other books and studies by **Bruce B. Miller**

When God Makes No Sense
A Fresh Look at Habakkuk

Big God in a Chaotic World
A Fresh Look at Daniel

Sexuality
Approaching Controversial Issues
with Grace, Truth and Hope

Same-Sex Marriage
A Bold Call to the Church
in Response to the Supreme Court's Decision

Your Church in Rhythm

Your Life in Rhythm
Your Life in Rhythm Study Guide

The Leadership Baton
The Leadership Baton Group Study Guide
(written with Rowland Forman and Jeff Jones)

Never the Same

A Fresh Look at the Sermon on the Mount
Matthew 5–7

BRUCE B. MILLER

McKinney, Texas

Dadlin Media is the publishing ministry of Dadlin ministries, an organization committed to helping people develop Wisdom for Life.

For more information please go to: http://BruceBMiller.com.

ISBN-10: 1-68316-012-6
ISBN-13: 978-1-68316-012-0

Printed in the United States of America

McKinney, TX 75070

BruceBMiller.com

Dedication

I dedicate this book to my grandchildren in the hope that you will each choose to follow Jesus with all your hearts, minds and souls. May Jesus' Sermon on the Mount guide your lives so they are never the same.

Contents

How to Benefit from this Book

You can read the eight chapters by themselves, but I encourage you to use the Study Guide based on The WISDOM Process© to gain even more insights from Jesus' Sermon on the Mount.

Because the Bible is more important to read than my thoughts on it, throughout the book we will direct you to read the relevant biblical passage.

The Bible is food for our souls. When we approach it prayerfully, the Spirit of God transforms our minds and blesses us with divine insights. Immersing yourself in the Word of God will grow you spiritually.

When we get alone to engage with God and focus our attention on understanding his Word, he speaks to us. Connecting in a group to discuss what you are learning will help you grow even more. Invite a friend to do the study with you. Join a group, or start one of your own and prepare for what God has in store!

Introduction

I invite you to a spiritual quest as we dive deep into the Sermon on the Mount. Open your heart to the Spirit, praying Jesus' kingdom vision becomes your vision for your life. The Sermon is only three chapters long. I encourage you to read it in its entirety every week as you study through it.

As the longest recorded talk by Jesus, the Sermon on the Mount is the most influential speech in the history of the world. Jesus turns most people's view of life upside down. Many are familiar with famous lines in the sermon such as: "Do unto others as you would have them do unto you," "Turn the other cheek," "Go the extra mile," and "Don't judge." Yet it's familiarity with these sayings that dulls our minds to what Jesus is really saying. We need to freshly hear Jesus.

You see, in his day Jesus' sermon shocked and offended his original audience. Therefore, if we are not shocked by his sermon, we may not really understand what Jesus is saying.

The overall point is this: Follow Jesus' kingdom vision and you will stand out as a bright light in this dark world, stand up when storms come, and step up to receive God's eternal reward. Jesus calls us to be all in, holding nothing back. You will never be the same!

CHAPTER ONE

You are the Light of the World

Matthew 5:1–16

What exactly is a New Year's resolution? Often merely a to-do list for the first week of January! Resolutions are tough to keep. More important than keeping New Year's resolutions is determining what resolutions we should set in the first place.

Twitter did a study of New Year's resolutions and according to an analysis of Tweets, found the following top three most popular resolutions:

1. Work out
2. Be happy
3. Lose weight

I think the first and third are supposed to make the middle one happen—but will they really?

Here's the real question we need to ask ourselves: What would be on Jesus' resolution list for us? What kind of life does Jesus call us to live?

Jesus gives us eight things to do to be blessed, classically called "Beatitudes"—a Latin word for "blessed." We generally don't find these on our own resolution lists. There's nothing wrong with the three goals on most people's lists, but those aren't the goals on Jesus' list. In fact, I wonder if any of us have any of Jesus' Beatitudes on our goal list—or have even considered putting them on our lists.

You see, the vision he gives—his kingdom vision—is quite different from how we ordinarily see the world. We need to pray for God to help us hear with fresh ears what Jesus has to say because he is presenting a new divine manifesto as the King. This is the new way we are to live. His original listeners were hanging on each word because Jesus' teachings were so different from what they had been taught.

Jesus paints a portrait of a Christlike life and models the vision he paints. He summons us to live a different kind of life, one that will bring incredible blessings now and forever; but few of us are seeking to live the vision he paints. We don't even see it, so it is not reflected in our resolutions.

Speaking with kingly authority, what Jesus teaches is so radical, so demanding, so uncompromising, so countercultural that many have attempted to water it down, to domesticate his message, to explain it away, to soften it so it will make sense to us.

Jesus' message is not about how to succeed in life—it's so much deeper than that. It is about how to live in his kingdom under his rule. And if we do so, we will find three amazing benefits:

1. We will stand out as a bright light in this dark world.
2. We will stand strong when storms come.
3. We will step up one day to receive God's eternal reward.

In this chapter, we dive into the preamble to his sermon comprised of eight Beatitudes followed by an amazing challenge and an awesome opportunity. Here's how it starts:

Matthew 5:1–2

Now when Jesus saw the crowds, he went up on a mountainside and sat down. His disciples came to him, and he began to teach them.

Notice the authority of Jesus. He went up on a mountain as Moses did centuries earlier. In a sense, his sermon is the "Torah of the Messiah."[1] Jesus is the new Moses bringing the "New Torah," the new way of living from God. He is the King, the priest, the prophet and lawgiver who came with authority to give us a new way to live.

The crowd gathered around Jesus eager to hear his fresh spiritual vision. I invite you to the same posture. Sit at Jesus' feet, eager to hear his message and hang on his every word, even when it is jarring, convicting and demanding. You will feel Jesus stepping on your toes in each chapter.

Therefore, pray to be prepared to hear what he has to say. Pray that his kingdom vision becomes your personal vision, as you become the person Jesus Christ calls you to be.

One word appears nine times: "blessed." If you follow Jesus' kingdom vision, God will bless you.

God will bless you

What does it mean to be "blessed"? People throw that term around all the time, usually in the context of getting extra money, a new job or something good happening to them. That's not really what it means. The Greek term cannot be reduced to happiness, based on "happenings" or circumstances. In Greek, *makarios,* (blessed) means fundamentally to be approved. There can be no higher blessing than to be approved by God, to have God's favor, which is not dependent on circumstances. We can be blessed regardless of our earthly circumstances, which might not be outwardly happy.

The term refers to someone who is to be congratulated. To be blessed is to experience the applause of heaven.[2] God's blessing is his applauding you. When you live the kind of life Jesus is describing, you win God's favor and approval. In our vernacular, he is saying, "Way to go!"[3] What could be better than hearing that from the King of Kings and Lord of lords, the God of the universe? Jesus tells us how we can gain God's applause by giving us eight qualities that describe the people receiving these blessings. These eight divine blessings can be yours if you live the way Jesus asks you to live.

Fundamentally, we need to aspire to be people who live "all in" for Christ, holding nothing back. We don't want to be people who are just playing church. We don't want to be a mile wide and an inch deep in our faith in God. If Jesus is who he said he is and the Word of God is true, then we need to be people who are all in for Jesus.

If you want to be all in and hold nothing back, the Sermon on the Mount tells us how to do it. These are our instructions for how to be all-in followers of Jesus Christ. The Beatitudes are not a scheme for self-improvement, for how to succeed in life; rather they are qualities of Jesus-like people. It is not the rich, the physically fit, the happy or the forceful who are truly blessed. It is the poor in spirit, the mourners and the meek who are blessed. As you read the Beatitudes, prayerfully consider which one God is drawing you to focus on.

Matthew 5:3–10

Blessed are the poor in spirit,
for theirs is the kingdom of heaven.
Blessed are those who mourn,
for they will be comforted.

Blessed are the meek,
for they will inherit the earth.
Blessed are those who hunger and thirst for righteousness,
for they will be filled
Blessed are the merciful,
for they will be shown mercy.
Blessed are the pure in heart,
for they will see God.
Blessed are the peacemakers,
for they will be called children of God.
Blessed are those who are persecuted because of righteousness,
for theirs is the kingdom of heaven.

We all need these qualities in our lives, but most of us don't make them our goals, and yet they are the qualities Jesus singles out for a blessed life. Ask God which one of the eight qualities he wants you to address most at this point in your life. The first is a clear starting point.

Beatitude 1

Blessed are the poor in spirit, for theirs is the kingdom of heaven.

Do any of us pray to be more "poor in spirit"? I doubt that was on anyone's resolution list. What does it mean to be "poor in spirit"?

"Poor in spirit" does not describe financial poverty or a low self-esteem. Jesus was not saying, "Blessed are the pathetic people or the wimps of the world." To be "poor in spirit" is to recognize our personal moral lack, our spiritual poverty apart from God.

Most people believe that we are essentially good. Our short-comings are simply exceptions to the rule. We can fix ourselves if we just keep our resolutions and live better lives. In truth, our problem is deeper than the fact that we just need to try harder. How many of us have tried harder and failed? It's not about setting better goals. If our problem was just keeping our resolutions, God would not have needed to send Jesus to save us. Our problem is so much deeper than that.

"Poor in spirit" is not a confession that we are insignificant, or personally without value, both of which are untrue. It is, rather, a confession that apart from Christ, our problem is that we are sinful and rebellious.[4] We are impoverished spiritually. We have a problem and it's worse than we know. Most of us don't want to recognize that. Instead we minimize and rationalize, telling ourselves, "I'm a fairly good person. I just mess up a little now and then." That is really denial.

The first step on the road to spiritual recovery is to admit you are powerless—that you have a problem you can't solve. You can't deal with all the harmful habits, hurts, behaviors and problems in your life. Good intentions are not enough. Will power is not enough. You need a power beyond your own. We must admit our need in order to be able to get the supernatural help to be free from the bondage of sin. If we don't realize our need and repent, we will never enjoy the blessings God has for us. The healing, the hope and the salvation that he has for us starts with a recognition that we have a problem.

We must become like the tax collector who was praying in the temple (in great contrast with the self-righteous Pharisee) and, according to Jesus:

Luke 18:13b

Would not even look up to heaven, but beat his breast and said, "God, have mercy on me, a sinner."

The tax collector was poor in spirit. Another model for poverty of spirit is the prodigal son, who ran away from home, but when he woke up and realized what he had done, he returned home to his father and confessed:

Luke 15:21

Father, I have sinned against heaven and against you. I am no longer worthy to be called your son.

If you are not yet a believer in Jesus, this is your starting place—you must realize that you need to be saved before you can experience salvation. Conviction precedes conversion. You must realize you need Jesus and understand that God sent Jesus to save you. Then when you trust in him, God gives you salvation. Shatter the illusion that you are sufficiently righteous to please God. Until you know how helpless and sinful you are, you can never see how worthy and glorious Christ is. Until you see your own poverty, you cannot see God's riches. It starts with being poor in spirit.

These Beatitudes are the foundation for a ministry called Celebrate Recovery. If you are dealing with addictive behavior, I would encourage you to get into a Christ-centered Celebrate Recovery program at a local church.

Expose yourself to the full glare of this Beatitude. Nothing is more uncomfortable than to discover what we thought was going to pass muster doesn't even get us in the front door. Maybe that's the Beatitude you need to focus on right now. The second Beatitude follows the first.

Beatitude 2

Blessed are those who mourn, for they will be comforted.

This is also a very unusual Beatitude. Few of us enjoy mourning, yet the truth is that spiritual poverty leads to godly sorrow. The philosophy of the world is to put on a happy face and smile, smile, smile. Don't get down on yourself. Look in the mirror and tell yourself that you are happy. But Jesus calls us to mourn. I'm fairly confident few of us set a goal to mourn more. Jesus is not talking about mourning over loss, being sad that someone died or that something bad happened to us.

Jesus is speaking of mourning over sin. He's talking about a godly sorrow. God mourns over our sin. We must also grieve over our sin—our individual sin, our sin as a community and the world's sin. Mourning over sin includes grieving over injustice, immorality, racism rampant across our world, and all sin which dishonors our God. We need to experience deep remorse over our sin and others' sin—even to the point of shedding tears. There is no comfort that can compare with what God gives to those who mourn.

What a different way to live—blessed are those who mourn. I can't get over the sense that as Christians in America today, we have a defective sense of sin. We are not poor in spirit and we don't mourn over sin. There is not enough sorrow for sin. We don't understand what Jesus is telling us. As Jesus-like mourners, we should mourn the greed, the cynicism, the perversion in our communities, and maybe we need to mourn that there aren't more mourners! I love the song lyric that says, "Break my heart for what breaks yours."[5]

I am convicted that I have not mourned enough over sin—mine and others. This mourning is the agonizing realization that it was *my* sin—*our* sins—that nailed Christ to the cross.

Those who mourn will be comforted because our Father is the God of all comfort. He comforts us with total forgiveness. That is what the gospel is all about: saving us from the horrendous guilt of our sin. If we never taste the sorrow of repentance, we will not feast on the comfort of salvation.

Have you ever felt deep remorse over your sins or the sins of others because they have dishonored God? Maybe God is convicting you to become poor in spirit or to mourn over sin, or it may be the next Beatitude that really grabs you.

Beatitude 3

Blessed are the meek for they will inherit the earth.

Again, this is not a very popular Beatitude. Our world's philosophy says only the strong survive, swim with the sharks, get tough, the route to success is to be aggressive, look out for number one. Who wants to put meekness on their resume? It is not a value that is honored. Nice guys usually finish last.

When I was in high school memorizing the Sermon on the Mount, I had an older aunt who said at a Thanksgiving dinner, "I don't want to be meek. That's terrible." I think she misunderstood meekness as being timid, being an indecisive person, really passive or a wimp. That's not what Jesus is talking about.

So what is Jesus-like meekness? Meekness is not a lack of backbone. Rather, the Greek term for meekness, *praus*, means, "the quality of not being overly impressed by a sense of one's self-importance, gentleness, humility, courtesy, considerateness."[6] Jesus was meek. Meekness is strength under control. It's the ability to endure insults and move on. Meekness is not being aggressive, seeking after our own agenda and our good. It's putting someone else first. As such, it is an incredible trait to have in our lives.

Meek people have a quiet steadiness about their lives in the midst of the upheaval because they are utterly yielded to God. It is freedom from pretension and the ability to endure injury, to turn the other cheek and go the extra mile. A meek person does not aggressively insist on their own rights. They control their emotions in the face of disappointing circumstances and behavior in others.

Meek people know they will "inherit the earth," meaning they will share in God's kingdom one day. Since they are not grabbing for more, they can be at peace with what they have and don't have, and they can enjoy what God provides, knowing what is to come. Would I envy your nice car or new house if I knew that my Father owned the city and I was the beneficiary of his will? One day God will give the earth to the meek. How are you doing with meekness? At home? In school? At work?

What do you really want? What do you desire so much that you can taste it? What do you really hunger after? Advertisers understand the power of hunger. But after a few days of feasting from the table of most advertised products, we realize we are just eating large bites of cotton candy and it really doesn't satisfy. God's answer is not to temper our desires, but to change the object of our desire. The fourth Beatitude addresses desire.

Beatitude 4

Blessed are those who hunger and thirst for righteousness for they will be satisfied.

Become addicted to righteousness. Jesus calls us to desire intensely those things that will really satisfy. Righteousness ultimately means being like the Lord Jesus Christ. Righteousness is that which corresponds to the will of God in our lives. It is what will satisfy. To be satisfied means to be filled to overflowing, having a full stomach. Righteousness brings satisfaction, but without wanting it, we will never get it.

The question is: How good do we want to be? To hunger and thirst for righteousness is the deep desire to be free even from the very desire for sin. Rather than wishing for one more drink, one more pill (over the prescription), one more puff, one more purchase or one more glance, the one who hungers after righteousness wants to get rid of sin. If we hunger and thirst for righteousness, we yearn to serve more, to give more and to love more because we want to be like Jesus.

Most people would say it's good to be a little righteous sometimes. They think it could be a good thing in moderation, but not a necessity, and not as important as food and drink. In contrast, a starving person knows nothing of moderation, but has a single, all-consuming obsession for food. Our obsession for righteousness should be just as strong and all-consuming.

Do you long for righteousness as a thirsty person longs for water? How intense is your hunger and thirst to obey God and to be like Jesus? Maybe this is the one Beatitude the Spirit of God is pressing on you, and the resulting blessing will be your utter satisfaction. If the first four Beatitudes have not rocked your world yet, take a look at the second set of four Beatitudes.

Beatitude 5

Blessed are the merciful, for they will be shown mercy.

The Roman Stoics called mercy a sickness of the soul. They saw it as weakness. The Greek word, *eleos*, means "kindness or concern expressed for someone in need."

Mercy sees someone else's pain, feels their hurt, and shares their emotions. They feel compassion and they do something about it. Mercy takes action. Merciful people give food to the hungry, comfort to the grieving, love to the rejected, forgiveness to the offender, and companionship to the lonely. Mercy shows the love of Jesus.

I want to be a person of mercy. This is the Beatitude where I have most keenly felt the Spirit of God's conviction. Often I wish I could be half as merciful as my wife, Tamara. The moment she hears someone has been in the hospital, she prays for them and offers to bring them a meal. I could not count the number of hurting people she has visited in their homes, in the hospital and in rehabilitation centers. She remembers their children, and the details of their illness or surgery. Of course, Jesus was the most merciful person. We need to be more like Jesus in the frequency and extent to which he showed mercy. When we know our need for mercy and then experience God's mercy poured out on us, we can show it to others.

What about you? How do you show mercy especially when you are striving for success in business, when you are in a hurry as a customer, when the other person makes a mistake or does something you think is stupid? The next Beatitude is equally challenging.

Beatitude 6

Blessed are the pure in heart, for they will see God.

The basic meaning of the Greek term *katharos* (purify) is to cleanse from dirt, filth and contamination. The Greek term was often used of metals that had been refined until impurities were removed. In that sense, purity means unmixed, unalloyed, unadulterated. A pure heart is undivided, no mixture of motives, but shows a single-minded passion for God. The person with an unclean heart cannot truly see God. Their heart is clouded by impurity. It is foggy and they are far away from him.

In the New Testament, the heart is not just a place of emotion, but is the center of who we are. We are to be pure inside. To be pure in heart is to be uncompromisingly dedicated to Jesus Christ! We are to be all in, sold out, holding nothing back, totally devoted to Jesus with no shadow of anything else that distracts us—pure in our hearts as we live for God.

This is the way to truly see God. Since we can't see something that is far away from us, to "see God" is to be near to him. Seeing God is perceiving, understanding and sensing who he really is. The reward of the undivided heart is a vision of God. I want so much to see God. Perhaps purity is the place God has for you to focus. Or perhaps it is being a peacemaker.

Beatitude 7

Blessed are the peacemakers,
for they will be called the children of God.

Peacemaking is a hallmark of God's children. Jesus is the supreme peacemaker who reconciles us to God through the cross.[7]

Biblically, "peace" means more than the absence of trouble. In this instance, "peace" echoes the Hebrew word, *Shalom*—all that is good for a person. It is actively getting engaged to bring reconciliation and healing, to bring peace. Being a peacemaker is more than being passive. It's more than not creating waves. A peacemaker speaks the truth gently and in love.

Peacemakers do more than just live peaceful lives; they actively seek to "make peace" through entering into the conflict to bring reconciliation, to end bitterness and strife between warring parties.[8] True peace is hard won. We must apologize. We must gently confront. We must forgive.

Peacemakers are not always "nice" or "tolerant;" rather, they take the initiative no matter who is at fault to actively bring peace. A peacemaker apologizes first, but also speaks the truth in love and says things as they are. Otherwise, there is no real peace, it's just fake—people smiling and covering it over.

How are you doing in being a peacemaker? Perhaps there is one person that the Spirit of God is bringing to your mind, a situation, where you need to be a peacemaker. That's what his followers do, make peace, and when we do, we will be "called children of God," those who are like our Father, the greatest peacemaker.

Beware that God's peacemakers will not always have peace in the world as Jesus makes clear in the eighth and last Beatitude. If you live this all-in kingdom life taught by Jesus, you *will* be persecuted.

Beatitude 8

Blessed are those who are persecuted for righteousness,
for theirs is the kingdom of heaven.

To call persecution a blessing is disturbing to us. But Jesus is not saying that you enjoy the mistreatment. There is a blessing in suffering for his sake that is incredibly rich and rare. You will have God's favor and God's approval.

This Beatitude rocks our world as to what a Christian looks like. We can wrongly view a Christian as a nice person who never offends anyone and is easy to get along with. But that's not what's going on here. Jesus was not the meek and mild Mr. Rogers of the children's television show, or Toby on "The Office."

If this Beatitude is true, the mature Christian is not praised by everybody. Jesus was at cross-purposes with the world and he offended a lot of people. They crucified him. If you are going to follow Jesus' kingdom vision living according to his way of life, you are going to be out of step with the world, but you are going to receive God's blessing—and that is worth it all.

We need to be careful that we do not claim to be suffering for Jesus during the many times we suffer because of our own sin and foolish choices. The Beatitude does not say, "Blessed are the offensive."

Many people around the world today are suffering for their faith in Jesus Christ, maybe more than at any time in history. Many in the world are being killed for their faith. We have already begun to face mild persecution in the United States.

In America, far too many Christians today are afraid of merely being ridiculed and that holds us back from being bold for Jesus. We don't worry that someone will punch us in the face because we are Christians or that we will be tortured, put in prison or killed. We just worry that someone might think we are a little radical.

If you live as an all-in Christ follower, your family and friends may ridicule you—"Well, you know he is a Christian, but he carries it a bit far." If you give your money to the church, some people will think you are crazy. When one of the couples in our church asked for a cashier's check to make a large donation, their banker questioned them. Generous giving to God is countercultural.

If we are going to live for Jesus, we have to expect there will be some kind of persecution. Although in America, what we face is so minor in comparison to the rest of the world, we still face opposition. And we should be bold enough to have someone think poorly of us. There is a blessing in that mild persecution. Let's go all out for Jesus, holding nothing back.

Which of these eight qualities that Jesus presents is God most impressing on your heart? If we follow Jesus' kingdom vision, God will bless us. In the next two verses, Jesus expands on the last Beatitude.

Jesus adds one more blessing and a great reward:

Matthew 5:11–12

Blessed are you when people insult you, persecute you and falsely say all kinds of evil against you because of me. Rejoice and be glad, because great is your reward in heaven, for in the same way they persecuted the prophets who were before you.

God does not tell us to rejoice in the mistreatment itself. The joy is not in the persecution and the insults. However, we can rejoice because our reward is great and because we stand in a heritage of godly people who were persecuted before us. It is an honor to suffer for Christ.

What should we expect in return for our commitment to Christ? Will he keep us healthy and protect our kids? Will he keep your car from being broken into? Will we become more prosperous than if we were less committed Christians?[9] God never makes those promises. In fact, just the opposite.

The Beatitudes are not a prescription for popularity. This isn't a program for how to succeed in life, make friends and influence them. This is how to live for Jesus.

If we follow Jesus' kingdom vision, we will be insulted and persecuted. In that mistreatment, we can rejoice because we have a greater reward. Following Jesus' vision will bring a great reward from God, an eternal reward. So follow Jesus' kingdom vision because God will bless you, reward you and do one more great thing for you. God will use you to help others honor him if you shine your light.

God will use you

In the last four verses of the introduction to the sermon, verses 13–16, we find our mission as Jesus' followers. Essentially, our mission is to be salty and bright.

Matthew 5:13–16

You are the salt of the earth. But if the salt loses its saltiness, how can it be made salty again? It is no longer good for anything, except to be thrown out and trampled underfoot.

[14]You are the light of the world. A town built on a hill cannot be hidden. [15]Neither do people light a lamp and put it under a bowl. Instead they put it on its stand, and it gives light to everyone in the house. [16]In the same way, let your light shine before others, that they may see your good deeds and glorify your Father in heaven.

Being Jesus' disciple is not merely a private matter between a person and God.[10] To be a Jesus follower means to carry on his mission, to be salt and light in the world.

Notice the word "you" is the first word in verses 13–14. *You* are salt and *you* are light. This is our identity as Christ followers. We are to be salty. If we are not living all-in lives for Jesus, then we are like tasteless salt. If our lives are bland, they will have no influence in the world. If we hide our light, it cannot illumine the darkness.

Jesus is the Light of the world and we are to uncover our lights so his brilliant light shines through us. Light is not simply a generic metaphor for moral influence, but an image of the gospel mission. Our task is to bring not just good to the world, but we are to bring the gospel to the world. Our mission is not simply to improve the world, but to live Jesus' kingdom vision. This is the mission of Jesus.

The picture of putting a lamp under a basket is a deliberate hyperbole meant to be humorous and ridiculous. Imagine all the lights go out in your house so everyone is in the dark. You get out a bright flashlight to help everyone see, but then you put it in a box and put a lid on it. How dumb. Now it will not help anyone. They might not even know you have a flashlight. Isn't this what we do in our lives? We hide the fact that we are Christ followers. We do not let our lights shine. Is your life like a searchlight beaming into the night or more like a flashlight in a box?[11]

Our bright words and salty actions should stand out in a rotten, dark world. Let people see your confidence in Jesus when everything is falling apart, your peace in the storm, your joy in depressing times. Talk to people about Jesus and invite people to your church. Be bold. He calls us to shine as a light on a hill.

■

The Sermon on the Mount is remarkable. It is Jesus' kingdom manifesto. This is the way we are to live. Will you follow Jesus' kingdom vision by living out these eight Beatitudes? What is God saying to you today? Which Beatitude is the Spirit pressing on your heart?

Maybe we need to revisit our "New Year's resolutions." More deeply, maybe we need to revisit our vision of a great life. What one step could you take to be more of an all-in Christ follower who holds back nothing? This week, what one person will you help to honor God? To whom will you shine your light?

Jesus calls us to be all in, holding nothing back. If we do so, we will discover a life full of blessing, now and eternally. We will bless many others. And most of all, we will bring honor to our Father in heaven.

▌

For further study on chapter 1, see page 109 for an Introduction followed by the Study Guide on page 113.

CHAPTER TWO

Go and Be Reconciled

Matthew 5:17–26

I was angry—angry at the National Football League (NFL) refs for overturning what I thought was an obvious and amazing catch by Dallas Cowboys' wide receiver Dez Bryant that could have changed the outcome of the National Football Conference divisional round playoff game against the Green Bay Packers in 2015. I was not the only person angry at perceived injustice. Sometimes anger at sporting events turns to violent rage. So much that we hire police officers at sporting events to protect ourselves from each other. It all starts with the parents in little league games.

Hate-filled anger is a major issue in our world, in our lives, and in our homes. For the first time in many years, a political protest song was nominated for song of the year at the 2015 Grammy Awards. The song and video, "Take Me to Church" by Hozier, disturbs me because it associates the church with homophobic violence of the worst kind. The video is full of hateful anger and violence.

On Christmas Day 2014, *Selma* was released, just before the fiftieth anniversary of the historic march. Quickly it became the number one movie in America. When my wife and I saw it, we were stunned by its power, pain and inspiration. Fifty years later, killings perceived as racially motivated are still occurring in such diverse places as Ferguson, Missouri and New York clearly revealing that we still have a long way to go in healing racism.

On January 11, 2015, the largest march in France since the end of World War II took place, with over 3.7 million attending including a huge variety of world leaders. They protested against the hate-filled, angry violence perpetrated the prior week on a Jewish supermarket and the offices of the French satirical magazine, *Charlie Hebdo,* in the name of religion. People were murdered in the name of Islam.

But the most common place for violence is still our homes. According to one report, "Between 2005 and 2010, 60 percent of all violent injuries in this country were inflicted by loved ones or acquaintances. And 60 percent of the time those victimizations happened in the home."[12] For a time in 2016, domestic violence took center stage in our media because Baltimore Raven running back Ray Rice attacked his wife and the nation responded with the "No More" campaign. No more silence on domestic violence.

Jesus Christ calls us to a different life, to be peacemakers in a world of hate. What would it look like for us to resist hate-filled anger and violence? Jesus tells us in the next part of the Sermon on the Mount. Our world desperately needs to hear Jesus' kingdom vision. And so do each of us.

Public schools close each year for Martin Luther King Day, when we remember a great reformer who stood against hate-filled violence. His "I Have a Dream" speech is one of the most well-known and revered in American history. He captured American imaginations when he said, "I have a dream that my four little children will one day live in a nation where they will not be judged by the color of their skin, but by the content of their character. I have a dream today!" King's speech helped propel the Civil Rights Movement, and still today motivates people of all colors to end hatred and pursue peace.

Jesus is the King of all kings and the Sermon on the Mount is his most famous speech. Jesus' message propelled the global Christian movement. Despite Martin Luther King's significant impact on his audiences, he did not possess the power to make his dream a reality. Only Jesus has the power to make his dream a reality for all who follow him. One day the King of Kings will end all racism, hate and violence.

Jesus shocked his original audience. Frankly, today we need to be shocked out of our spiritual slumber. The overall message of the Sermon is to follow Jesus' kingdom vision so we will never be the same. Pray that God will show you what you need to see in this passage where Jesus defines greatness in his kingdom and then gives a specific example. You will be great in Jesus' kingdom if you follow Jesus' commands and help others follow them.

Follow Jesus' Commands

In Matthew 5:17, Jesus starts with a theological and practical issue. What are we to do with the Old Testament? Is it still valid today? In other words, can we eat bacon? [I ask this as a bacon lover.] In his day, Jesus was accused of being anti-law because of things he did, such as healing people on the Sabbath. Jesus had the audacity to claim that as the Messiah, he fulfilled the Old Testament law in a way that transforms it without abolishing it. He claimed that the entire Old Testament was looking forward to him.

These next few verses are crucial to understanding how to read the Old Testament and are key to interpreting the rest of the Sermon on the Mount. Jesus explains how to read the Old Testament through him and in the process, defines greatness in his kingdom program.

Matthew 5:17–26

Do not think that I have come to abolish the Law or the Prophets; I have not come to abolish them but to fulfill them. [18] *For truly I tell you, until heaven and earth disappear, not the smallest letter, not the least stroke of a pen, will by any means disappear from the Law until everything is accomplished.* [19] *Therefore anyone who sets aside one of the least of these commands and teaches others accordingly will be called least in the kingdom of heaven, but whoever practices and teaches these commands will be called great in the kingdom of heaven.* [20] *For I tell you that unless your righteousness surpasses that of the Pharisees and the teachers of the law, you will certainly not enter the kingdom of heaven.*

People have drifted to two extremes in how to understand Jesus' relationship to the Old Testament. The infamous second-century heretic Marcion basically said we should ignore the Old Testament. He argued that it had been superseded by the New Testament, so it was no longer valid. Following in Marcion's footsteps today, many Christians wrongly ignore the Old Testament. But God says that **all** Scripture is God-breathed and profitable for us (2 Timothy 3:16–17).

On the other hand, the Coalition of Torah Observant Messianic Congregations believes that the Old Testament law continues to be in force today. They believe that we should still follow the Old Testament laws, including obeying the dietary laws such as not eating pork and keeping the Jewish festivals such as Hanukkah. But the New Testament frees us from those laws. Jesus neither simply reaffirms the law nor does he dismiss it. So what is Jesus saying? The right interpretation hinges on the key words "fulfill," and "accomplish." Jesus completes or metamorphosizes God's permanent word.

Jesus Completes

The phrase, "the law or the prophets," is a way of referring to the entire Old Testament. In Jesus Christ there is continuity and discontinuity with the Old Testament. The law continues, as Jesus says, until heaven and earth pass away and until all is accomplished, but that does not mean the law continues *unchanged*. The law is fulfilled in Jesus, but that does not mean that the law ends in Jesus as if it no longer has validity or value. Rather, Jesus completes the law. He is its goal so that in him it is fully realized, accomplished and re-interpreted.

The Old Testament points to Christ and blossoms in Christ. The law was partial and provisional. Jesus is full. The law was the acorn and Jesus is the tree. It's like the Old Testament is the architectural drawings and Jesus is the building. The law and prophets were black and white pencil sketches, and Jesus Christ is the full-color painting. The painting fills those sketches full. As a baby grows up to be a full grown adult, so the Old Testament grows into Christ, completed by Jesus.

We read the Old Testament through the lens of Jesus who metamorphosizes it. Metamorphosis is a profound change in the form of an organism, such as in its life history from a caterpillar to a butterfly. Jesus metamorphosizes the law. It remains the authoritative Word of the living God, but it is transformed in Jesus, the one to whom it always pointed. The law is not done away with, but remains in effect in a more profound way. Some aspects are no longer directly applicable, such as the dietary law, sacrifices and festivals, but they still have value in how they point to Christ. Far from being opposed to the law, Jesus brings it to fruition, revealing the deeper implications in the law.

In the Sermon, Jesus gives six examples of how he fulfills the law. We will now look at the first example. Jesus overturns faulty interpretations by Jewish religious leaders of his day and unfolds implications that were in the law all along. How can you be great in Jesus' kingdom? You are great in Jesus' kingdom if you obey his commands and teach others.

Obey and teach

To be great in Jesus' kingdom, we need to obey and teach his commands. Follow Jesus yourself and then help others to find and follow Jesus. But Jesus adds a kicker that knocks us all out:

Matthew 5:20

For I tell you that unless your righteousness surpasses that of the Pharisees and the teachers of the law, you will certainly not enter the kingdom of heaven.

The teachers of the law and the Pharisees were the most devout people, those who followed the law scrupulously. They would be like Orthodox Jews today. In Christian circles, it would be like pointing to Billy Graham, Mother Theresa, or Martin Luther and saying, "You've got to be much, much better!"

Jesus' point is not that we score higher than the Pharisees on the entrance exam. Instead Jesus is talking about a qualitatively different kind of righteousness: from *don't murder* to *don't be angry*. He says we mess up if we even set aside one of the least commands. You cannot enter Jesus' kingdom unless you have surpassing righteousness. This is an impossible ideal. So who can enter the kingdom? Answer: No one.

Realize Jesus is speaking at the start of his ministry. The cross, resurrection and sending of the Spirit are not in view yet. From the viewpoint of the entire New Testament, we can see that this is a starting point of the gospel. No one can keep all the law. No one can be perfectly righteous. Jesus is the only one who did it. He fulfills the law on our behalf. The promise of the gospel is that God will make us righteous in Jesus.

Once you trust in Jesus and have the Holy Spirit in your heart, how can you be great in Jesus' kingdom, all in, holding nothing back? You obey his commands and teach others. This is Jesus' basic framework for being his follower. We are to be people helping people find and follow Christ. We can check our progress spiritually by answering two questions: What next step are you taking to follow Christ better? And who are you helping to follow Christ? Who have you met with for coffee and talked about God? Have you shared something from your personal Bible reading with another person?

Having given us the basic framework for kingdom life, Jesus now gives a specific example, the first of six. Each of the six follows the same basic pattern: *You have heard that it was said . . . but I say to you.* Look at Matthew 5:21 for the first example. I have summarized Jesus' point as don't do this, but do this. Don't get angry and insult people, but do reconcile. Let's look at the "don'ts" first.

Matthew 5:21–22

You have heard that it was said to the people long ago, "You shall not murder, and anyone who murders will be subject to judgment." [22] But I tell you that anyone who is angry with a brother or sister will be subject to judgment. Again, anyone who says to a brother or sister, "Raca" is answerable to the court. And anyone who says, "You fool!" will be in danger of the fire of hell.

Jesus is saying if you verbally insult people, you will be sent to fiery hell. No wonder he offended people. You might be offended right now. Most of his audience was. Mental murder and verbal murder will be subject to God's judgment as will physical murder. Jesus is saying don't get hatefully angry and insult people.

Don't get angry and insult

Throughout the sermon, we will see Jesus over and over use graphic images and outrageous illustrations to make his point. From road-rage to religious-rage to racial-rage, we are soaked in angry hate that leads to violence and murder. Just read the comments on blogs, especially political rants. Watch the latest news on any given day. It starts in our homes with brothers killing brothers, echoing Cain and Abel over and over again, more blood spilled, more blood crying out to God for justice. Some of the people in the crowd around Jesus were growing in their anger against him, and would later insult him and finally kill him.

Let's start with our own hearts. Ask the Spirit of God to convict you. Where is anger the biggest problem for you? In your home? In traffic? In your office? On social media? Revisit the last time you were furious, really ticked off. Starting a Facebook post, "I just need to rant," might not be good. Just stop. Have you ever wished someone were dead? We cannot escape the truth that we are all murderers. We have all murdered others in our thoughts and with our tongues. We have committed mental murder. And what is the result of mental murder?

Mental murder

Anger is the root and heart of murder and mental murder results in divine judgment. I can hear the quick objection that not all anger is sin. After all, we have examples in the Bible where God the Father is angry and Jesus is too. He even called some people fools (Matthew 23:17). In Ephesians 4:26, Paul says we are to be angry but not sin. There is righteous anger. Yet Jesus is not talking about righteous anger here, but selfish anger. Jesus is not talking about the anger that leads to reform, but anger that leads to violence. Anger over personal affronts—that I did not get my way. Honestly, the vast majority of human anger is sinful. If you are going to follow Christ, you must get rid of unrighteous anger. You must get rid of not only mental murder, but also verbal murder—insults.

Verbal murder

Verbal murder results in divine judgment. In the media today, you get people to read your blog or listen to your show by shouting harsh comments. People rain down curses on each other over the slightest offense. Does this happen in your home? In your marriage, what names have you called each other? Have you verbally murdered each other? What have you said to each other in anger? Don't think anger is a valid excuse for foul language. Words can be murderous. They maim souls. Words kill. We talk about character assassination. This happens every day in Starbucks as people gossip.

The first word Jesus mentions is "raca," a quasi-swear word in Aramaic, which probably meant something like empty-headed or "idiot." How many times have you called someone an idiot? I'm not sure I can count that high. The second word, "fool" is *mōros,* from which we get our word *moron*. The point is not to simply avoid these two specific words, but rather to avoid verbal murder, sparked by hateful anger.

What is the consequence for verbal murder, for insults and slurs? The severe consequence Jesus gives is totally unexpected and utterly shocking. You will be sent to fiery hell. We have all committed mental and verbal murder sometime in our lives. Most of us are mass murderers, verbally and mentally. So we all deserve to go to hell. That's why we need Jesus and the gospel. Where is anger the biggest problem for you? With whom is it the biggest issue?

Let's move to the positive, which is even harder. Jesus does not say we have succeeded when we have removed all unrighteous anger and verbal insults. He reverses the situation with two brief stories of a brother and an adversary:

Matthew 5:23–26

Therefore, if you are offering your gift at the altar and there remember that your brother or sister has something against you, [24] leave your gift there in front of the altar. First go and be reconciled to them; then come and offer your gift.

[25] Settle matters quickly with your adversary who is taking you to court. Do it while you are still together on the way, or your adversary may hand you over to the judge, and the judge may hand you over to the officer, and you may be thrown into prison. [26] Truly I tell you, you will not get out until you have paid the last penny.

Jesus pushes deeper into our souls; not only must we avoid mental and verbal murder—that is not enough. If we are even aware that someone has something against us, we should take the initiative to reconcile with them.

Reconcile with people

Reconciliation is difficult and costly. We are to repair damage. As we saw in the Beatitudes, we are called to be peacemakers. Jesus describes two brief situations: of a brother in worship, and of an adversary on the way to court. In the first situation, his point is that if you remember your brother has something against you, you should leave worship and go be reconciled.

Situation 1: You remember your brother has something against you
Priority: Leave worship and go be reconciled

Notice Jesus is not talking about you being offended by someone, but rather, you are aware that another person is upset with you. Jesus says it is a high priority that you reconcile. Reconciliation is so important you should leave your gift at the altar to first go be reconciled and then come present your gift. Reconciliation precedes worship.

The scene is almost comic. It takes about three days to get back from Jerusalem to Galilee, where most of Jesus' hearers lived. Picture someone leaving their live sacrificial sheep, walking three days back home, reconciling with his friend and then walking three days back to present the sheep he left. Jesus is exaggerating to make the point.

The graphic illustration is designed to grab our attention. It's hard to worship with anger in your heart or even with the awareness that someone else is angry with you. What relationship comes to your mind? With whom do you need to reconcile? Is there someone you need to talk with? Someone in your life that you know is upset with you? What about someone you live with or in your family? Maybe you need to deal with internal racism. In Jesus' second illustration with the adversary, his point is that when your adversary has a legal dispute with you, come to agreement quickly.

Situation 2: Your adversary has a legal dispute against you
Urgency: Come to agreement quickly

In the judicial system of Jesus' day, debtors in a legal dispute could be incarcerated until the debt was paid. Jesus is doing more than giving practical advice here. He is making a point. We should not delay in reconciling. When you leave food in the car, it rots. If you do not get rid of a tumor, it will grow. Once time goes by, people harden and forget the details of even why they got so upset. It becomes more difficult and awkward to talk about as months and years go by. So, what's the right time? Sooner rather than later. Do not put it off.

To settle matters means to make friends with or to be in agreement with someone. Martin Luther King said, "Returning violence for violence multiplies violence, adding deeper darkness to a night already devoid of stars.... Hate cannot drive out hate: only love can do that. Love is the only force capable of transforming an enemy into a friend."[13] What relationship do you need to reconcile before you go to your next worship service?

Jesus' overall point in the Sermon is that we should follow his kingdom vision. We should be all in, holding nothing back. In this passage, he is telling us that we can be great in Jesus' kingdom by obeying and teaching his commands: specifically, by avoiding hateful anger in our minds and words, and instead reconciling with people as an urgent priority. Our passage gives us a few important principles for reconciliation. Make it a priority—leave worship. Take the initiative—go to the person. And don't delay—do it quickly. The way to be great is to obey what Jesus commands and teach others to do the same. In other words, Jesus wants each of us to answer two simple, profound questions: What's your next step to follow Christ? And who are you helping to follow Christ?

▌

For further study on chapter 2, see page 123.

CHAPTER THREE

Let Your Yes Be Yes

Matthew 5:27–37

Jesus addresses three issues that are huge problems in our society and in our own families: lust, divorce and lying.

So many people lie to us so much of the time that we have little trust left. We don't trust politicians from any party. We do not trust lawyers. We don't trust salespeople's claims for their products. We don't trust the media or anyone in authority because they have lied so many times.

More sadly, we struggle to trust those we live with. Lies have eroded our marriages, damaged our children's trust and hurt our friends. Jesus paints a kingdom vision of truth. What if, as Christ's followers, we did not lie? What if all believers always spoke the truth in every sphere of our lives? What if you could trust every word that any Christian spoke? What amazing families we would have, how we would be trusted in business!

The second issue Jesus speaks to is divorce. Our day is very different from a few decades ago. All 50 states in America have no-fault divorce. Legally, divorce is relatively easy, and there is no social stigma to overcome. And yet we know the intense, lifelong pain of divorce. So many young adults have felt so much pain from their parents' divorces that they do not even want to get married out of fear that they too will get divorced, so they just live together. What if among followers of Jesus, there were no divorces? What if everyone who got married, stayed married, even when it got hard?

The third issue Jesus addresses is lust, obviously a giant issue in our hyper-sexualized culture. With pornography of the worst kind available on any device with Internet access, we rightfully fear for our children. Over Christmas with my adult kids home, I watched several movies they wanted to see, including a comedy from a few years ago whose edited version I had seen on television, but not the unedited version. I was horrified at the sexual crudity depicted as humor in the unedited version. In recent years, smart phones and social media have become new platforms for lust, from sexting to emotional affairs on Facebook.

Researchers are now tracking "digital infidelity" or "remote infidelity" through social media. A study at the University of Indiana reported Facebook users frequently use the site to keep up with "back burners," people who they could connect with romantically just in case the current husband or wife does not work out.[14] We should not have back burners! Instead, what if we followed Jesus' kingdom vision to stay pure? What if we were the kind of people who took drastic measures to avoid lust?

In the last chapter, I shared that most of us are mass murderers in terms of mental and verbal murder through anger and insults. In this next passage, Jesus will make a similar statement about lust. Get prepared to be convicted by the Spirit of God. You may feel crushed with guilt over your lust, your divorce or your lies. You may feel incredible pain and regret. Much of our guilt in this area is probably deserved.

Now in the third chapter, unpacking this convicting sermon by Jesus, like me you may have experienced so much conviction that you need to take time for confession and receiving God's grace. Like me, you clearly see you have sinned. At the end of the chapter, I encourage you to spend some time alone with God: to confess, to receive God's forgiveness and then to freshly devote yourself to following Jesus Christ. It is right to be convicted, but God does not want us to wallow in guilt. He wants us to soar in the gospel of Jesus that sets us free from condemnation.

In our passage, Jesus calls us to follow him by living a life characterized by three traits: purity, commitment and truthfulness, so we shine as bright lights in a dark world full of lust, divorce and lies. Jesus is not just giving moral commands. He is unveiling a whole new way of being human.[15] This is the real, good life. First, Jesus calls us to stay pure in our hearts: no lust.

Stay pure in your heart: no lust

Jesus says:

Matthew 5:27–28

> *You have heard that it was said, "You shall not commit adultery." But I tell you that anyone who looks at a woman lustfully has already committed adultery with her in his heart.*

Jesus cuts us to the soul with truth that applies to men and women. If we are honest with ourselves about our own lust, that truth should bring us to poverty of spirit, a realization that we are helpless sinners in desperate need of the grace of God. With pornography, romance novels that glamorize adultery, flirting in person and on the Internet, we are a mess.

In our sexualized culture, Jesus' standard seems so high. Perhaps you object, "But no one can avoid looking. Temptation is not sin." True, the first look is not sin. The temptation is not sin. It's the lustful look. It's when the fantasy begins. It is the look to desire, to have, when you give yourself to mental arousal. Lust is mental adultery, whether with a live person, pornography or romantic fantasy. If we are honest, nearly all of us are mental adulterers. And we've had much more than a one-time affair. We have committed serial mental adultery. How in the world can we get lust out of our lives? Jesus says we must take radical action. It is better to lose your eye and your hand than to nurture lustful thoughts?

Better to lose your eye and your hand

Jesus says:

Matthew 5:29–30

> *If your right eye causes you to stumble, gouge it out and throw it away. It is better for you to lose one part of your body than for your whole body to be thrown into hell. And if your right hand causes you to stumble, cut it off and throw it away. It is better for you to lose one part of your body than for your whole body to go into hell.*

He uses hyperbole to make the point that radical action is required to root lust out of our hearts. Obviously a person with one eye and one hand can still lust. Jesus did not mean that we are literally to rip out our eyeballs and amputate our hands. The point is that radical surgery is required to deal with lust. We can't play around with it. We can't take half measures. We must hate lust, crush it, dig it out. There will be pain and tears and blood. We have to get drastic. You may need to sever a relationship. You may need to cut a cord, pull out a plug, cancel a subscription, or throw something in the trash. What's on your Kindle? You may need to cut out a favorite activity, a place you like to go. Your action needs to be decisive and it will likely be painful. You must ruthlessly, even savagely, tear out and cut off whatever feeds lust. You may de-friend someone or cut off access to their Facebook feed.

Jesus says to gouge out your eye if it causes you to stumble. I think "stumble" is too soft a translation. Jesus is saying that lust can lead to moral corruption, what we might today call sexual addiction, and worse it can lead to spiritual apostasy. It grieves me to think of dear friends whose sexual sin led them to deny that they are even Christians any more. Lust can wreck your life, destroy you and those you love. Should not righteousness before God be worth more to us than sinful sexual pleasure that will hurt us in the end?

Jesus says it is better to lose a part of your body than for your whole body to be thrown into hell. Frankly, I do not enjoy even writing the word "hell," but this is the second time in a row that Jesus says it. I cannot ignore it. Apart from Jesus Christ, sin leads to death and eventually to hell.

Let's get specific. What is the Spirit of God convicting you to get rid of? In my life, my wife Tamara has the code for our television to protect me from myself. There are many movies I cannot watch unless she puts in the code. I use Covenant Eyes, a program that sends a report of every site I've visited on the Internet. The report goes to Tamara, an elder and an accountability partner as well as to one of my adult sons.

What do you need to gouge out? An old friend on Facebook with whom you once were romantic? A cable subscription, certain shows, books, magazines or a relationship? The point is not to be a legalist; that would mean you are imposing your standards on others. Rather, the point is to get as radical as Jesus tells us to be by "cutting off our hand." Maybe for you the best step is to go to a Christ-based recovery program such as those available at many local churches. From purity, Jesus moves to commitment. His second point is to stay committed to your spouse: no divorce.

No divorce

Notice that divorce comes right between the issues of lust and lying, which destroy many marriages. There would be less divorce if there were less lust and lying. Jesus says:

Matthew 5:31–32

It has been said, "Anyone who divorces his wife must give her a certificate of divorce." But I tell you that anyone who divorces his wife, except for sexual immorality, makes her the victim of adultery, and anyone who marries a divorced woman commits adultery.

These verses have been misread in ways that have created tremendous, unnecessary guilt for many people. The vast majority of people reading this chapter have experienced divorce either personally or in their immediate family, so it is an incredibly emotionally charged topic. I have walked with many through these tough waters.

Jesus' focus is on marriage, not on divorce. He is not giving reasons for divorce, but calling his followers to lifelong marriage. We make vows for as long as we both shall live, not for as long as it makes sense, for as long as we are happy together, or for as long as our needs are being met. As one person said, "Running out of romance provides no reason for running out of a marriage."[16] Of course, God does not want us to have awful marriages either. It is not pleasing to God to have a marriage filled with bitterness. But the answer is not to sever the marriage commitment. Marriage is a commitment so firm that when the going gets rough, you will stay committed. The gospel summons us to become peacemakers and agents of reconciliation,[17] including in our marriages.

To understand what Jesus is saying, we need to know the cultural background. In Matthew 5, Jesus is referring to Deuteronomy 24 where Moses gave provision for a certificate of divorce. Various Jewish teachers argued over grounds for divorce. There were three main schools of thought on divorce, ranging from the most conservative Shammai who said only adultery is a cause, to Hillel who said burning dinner was cause enough, to Aquiba who said finding a more beautiful woman was a good enough reason. After sharing this with my wife Tamara, she said, "So if your husband gets old, fat and hairy, you can leave him?" To which I said, "No. That is not what the Bible is saying"—and I am thankful.

Jesus goes beyond dispute over the grounds of divorce to focus on the sanctity of marriage. Jesus never commands divorce, but only permits it if all attempts at reconciliation have failed. Ancient Jews (like Greeks and Romans) almost universally agreed that lawful divorce granted a person the right to remarry. So Jesus' words would almost certainly have been taken as permission for remarriage when divorce was permitted, such as after marital unfaithfulness.[18]

What does Jesus mean by saying that divorce and remarriage cause a woman to become an adulteress? What if you marry a divorced woman? Does that mean for the rest of your life that you are living in persistent adultery? This is a place where people have lived in unnecessary guilt. There is no indication in the rest of the Bible that a second marriage, even following an illegitimate divorce, is seen as permanently adulterous. Life is really messy because of sin. Wherever you are today, whatever you have done before, the point is that from this day forward, you should faithfully follow Jesus. If you are married, be faithful to your current spouse. If you are single, live a celibate life.

Jesus does give an exception for divorce. What does Jesus mean by "except for marital unfaithfulness"? The Greek word is *porneia.*

Except for porneia

Porneia refers broadly to sexual immorality, including fornication, adultery, prostitution, incest and other sexual perversions. It's the word from which we get our word "pornography." Sometimes wives ask if they can get divorced because their husband watches pornography, in effect saying, "Jesus said that lust is adultery so my husband has committed adultery and I have a biblical escape clause to get a divorce." If every wife whose husband lusted has grounds for divorce, then every woman has grounds because close to 100 percent of us husbands are guilty of lust. The whole direction of that thinking is unbiblical. You should be looking for reasons to stay in your marriage, not ways to get out. Even if your spouse commits physical adultery, that does not mean you should get a divorce. The first approach should be reconciliation. If your spouse persists in adultery, then divorce may be the best option. If your spouse repents and is trying to change, then do all you can to reconcile.

In the bigger biblical picture, what does God say about marriage and divorce? Obviously I have to be very brief here and not write another book inside this book. Married people should stay married if at all possible. Divorce is not desirable. However, sometimes divorce is the best of the bad options. Jesus gives an exception for adultery and Paul gives an exception for abandonment. I believe physical abuse is also grounds. Anyone who divorces for biblical reasons is free to get remarried, but it is not necessary to remarry. Singleness is a great life.

Many divorced people feel uncomfortable in church. You might feel like you have a scarlet "D" on your forehead. You wonder if you will be treated as a second-class person, as dirty. That is not the case in a healthy church. You are accepted and forgiven by God. God loves you. Christ died for you. There is no sin that knocks you out of serving Christ for life. There is forgiveness and restoration in Jesus Christ.

So how do you respond? If you feel convicted by the Spirit of God, you may need to confess. Perhaps you divorced wrongly. God forgives. Perhaps you are contemplating divorce and you are convicted that your reasons don't hold biblical water. Recommit to your marriage. Just because he or she is not meeting your needs, or you have fallen out of love, does not mean you have cause to end a marriage. Maybe you are a single person considering marriage, or a student with plans for marriage far in the future. You need to settle today that when you get married, it will be for life. Divorce will never be an option for you. Don't get married with an escape clause. If you are living in unnecessary guilt, let it go. Accept God's forgiveness in Jesus. Then get about serving God. Don't listen to the devil lying to you, telling you that you are not good enough to serve God.

Let's consider the third trait of a Christ follower: truthfulness. Not only are followers of Jesus characterized by purity and commitment, but also by truthfulness. Stay true to your word: no lies.

No lies

On the surface, verses 33–37 could sound like the topic is oaths, but below the surface, the issue is simply telling the truth. Jesus says:

Matthew 5:33–37

> *Again, you have heard that it was said to the people long ago, "Do not break your oath, but fulfill to the Lord the vows you have made." But I tell you, do not swear an oath at all: either by heaven, for it is God's throne; or by the earth, for it is his footstool; or by Jerusalem, for it is the city of the Great King. And do not swear by your head, for you cannot make even one hair white or black. All you need to say is simply "Yes" or "No"; anything beyond this comes from the evil one.*

The Old Testament allowed for oaths and vows, and commanded that they be taken very seriously. However, Jewish teachers had developed an elaborate system of rules about which kind of oaths you really had to keep and which ones you could break because they did not involve God's name. It got to the point of silliness. For example, one rabbi says that if you swear by Jerusalem, you are not bound by your vow, but if you swear toward Jerusalem, then you are bound by your vow.[19] In other words, their system had legalized telling lies.[20] Jesus' point is quit evil word games.

Quit evil word games

One reason we create contracts is that we are such liars. It's the adult version of the child saying, "It does not count because I had my fingers crossed." Since a person's word or handshake cannot be trusted, we complicate daily life with contracts of all kinds. Jesus is not suggesting that all oaths are wrong. He himself testified under oath in his trial. Some people take these verses in an overly literal way that creates a new legalism, as if, for example, you should not say the Pledge of Allegiance or swear on a Bible in a courtroom. This is not Jesus' point. The point is that your yes should mean yes and your no should mean no. There is no need for more than that because Jesus' followers are truthful. No one has to say, "Cross my heart and hope to die." No need to pinky swear.

As a Jesus follower, your word should be as good as a signed contract. Anything beyond this comes from the evil one, who is Satan, otherwise known as the father of lies. The sad truth is that most of us lie a lot. Many times we hardly even think of them as lies. How about exaggerating a story to make yourself look good? How big was that fish? How about stretching the truth in business to sell your product or hiding the truth to reduce the downsides? How about lies to get out of trouble? "I never got your message; I was just kidding; I didn't hear you; We'll keep it on file; I'm sorry, I've got plans that day." Do you cheat on tests, taxes, job applications, or your resume?

Not long ago, once again, I repeated something I've done way too many times in our marriage. I said, "I'll be home at 6:30 for dinner," and then I played one more racquetball game, which caused me to get home later. Dinner was cold and Tamara was justifiably hot. I need to be a man of my word. If you are a parent, do you keep your word to your kids? Are you at their game when you say you will be?

It is good to be convicted of sin. Sin grieves God. But we should not wallow in conviction. Conviction should rightly lead to confession. We receive God's gracious forgiveness in his amazing grace. Then we consecrate ourselves to follow Christ. Jesus' point in this passage is that we are to obey Christ by living a life characterized by three traits: purity, commitment and truthfulness. No lust, no divorce and no lies. If we have these traits, we will shine our lights in a dark world. Imagine if each of us stayed pure in our hearts, stayed committed to our spouses and stayed true to our word, always. The impact would be huge. Our lives would be bright lights.

So how do we respond? Let me recommend that you *welcome the Holy Spirit's conviction*, then *confess your sin to our gracious Father*, then *consecrate yourself to follow Jesus Christ*. We are all guilty of sin, whether that be lust, divorce, lies or others. That's why Jesus came. Jesus came to live a perfect life so he could die for us. He is the only one who has lived a totally righteous life. He paid for our sin on the cross. Forgiveness and deliverance from guilt is found in Jesus. Trust in Jesus to forgive you. He is the only one who can. Jesus is the way to God.

Once we become his followers, Jesus calls us to a new kind of life, one that he gives us power to live by his Holy Spirit, who changes us from the inside out. The Sermon on the Mount is not a new set of rules, but a description of a new kind of person. As a follower of Jesus, God does not want us to live in guilt, but to live in forgiveness.

God stands ready to forgive you and heal you. I invite you to talk to God. Receive his grace, his total forgiveness. Let go of your guilt. God is faithful. God, our gracious Father, stays faithful to his compassion, faithful to his mercy and grace. He is ready to wash you clean with his grace in Jesus Christ.

A prayer of confession

> *God, I confess my sin to you. Thank you for forgiving me. I praise you for your forgiveness. You have set me free. God, thank you for your faithful love and grace. Amen.*

To consecrate means to devote or dedicate yourself. I invite you to freshly consecrate yourself to follow Christ. Consecrate yourself to stay pure in your heart, committed to your spouse and true to your words. Maybe you need to take drastic action to gouge out something.

■

For further study on chapter 3, see page 131.

CHAPTER FOUR

Turn the Other Cheek

Matthew 5:38–48

Revenge.

Revenge forms the fundamental plot for many action movies. The bad guy hurt the girl and that was his big mistake. "I'll be back," says Arnold in the *Terminator*. Clint Eastwood says, "Go ahead, make my day."

Revenge weaves into the main theme for thousands of songs. In 1966, Nancy Sinatra hit number one singing, "These boots are made for walking, and that's just what they'll do. One of these days these boots are gonna walk all over you." Who could forget Carrie Underwood's *Before He Cheats*, "I dug my key into the side of his pretty little souped-up four-wheel drive, carved my name into his leather seats. I took a Louisville slugger to both headlights, I slashed a hole in all four tires."

Sadly, we have experienced and dished out revenge in our own relationships. We make each other pay in a terrible cycle of getting back at each other by what we do or do not do. In families, it happens between siblings as kids, and as adults as well. There is the infamous restaurant revenge of the waiter who having been mishandled by you, contaminates your food before he serves it to you. From the playground to NFL stadiums, we want to make the other person pay for what they did to us. We want them to regret they ever hurt us.

Jesus calls us to a much higher way of living. The way of his kingdom soars above revenge. He calls us to a divine love for those who have done us wrong. Imagine if rather than thinking about how to get even, we dreamed about how to bless people who hurt us.

Jesus challenges our basic tendencies of self-protection and selfishness. In Matthew 5:38, far from calling us to retaliation, Jesus commands us to bless and to love. In the first of two sections in this passage, Jesus calls us to bless evildoers: no resistance.

Bless evildoers: no resistance

Jesus will quote an old saying and then take us to a much higher place:

Matthew 5:38–42

You have heard that it was said, "Eye for eye, and tooth for tooth." But I tell you, do not resist an evil person. If anyone slaps you on the right cheek, turn to them the other cheek also. And if anyone wants to sue you and take your shirt, hand over your coat as well. If anyone forces you to go one mile, go with them two miles. Give to the one who asks you, and do not turn away from the one who wants to borrow from you.

The Old Testament limited punishment to that which matched the severity of the crime, and no more. The point was to eliminate escalation. Jesus presents a totally different approach, giving good in response to evil.

Historically, the line, "Do not resist an evil person," has caused confusion. Does Jesus mean that no one should serve as a police officer, whose job is to resist evildoers? Should no one serve as a soldier in a country's armed forces? These are misapplications of Jesus' point because Jesus is speaking in the context of personal offense. It is fine and noble to serve as a police officer or a solider. A country should defend its citizens. Jesus stood for justice and defended the poor from abuse.

Mahatma Gandhi and Martin Luther King used Jesus' words to support their nonviolent resistance. But here's the problem: Jesus is teaching against more than violent resistance. He says we should not resist at all, not even nonviolently, not even legally. In fact, rather than resisting, he calls us to actively bless evildoers. Jesus does not shy away from calling certain people evil. There are bad people who will insult you, abuse you and hurt you. Then he calls us to generously bless those very people. We answer evil with good.

We can understand Jesus' point better by looking at each of the five different life situations he paints. These are not a new set of rules, but pictures to help us see what it looks like to live as Jesus' followers. His words strike at the very core of human selfishness. Jesus calls his followers to break the human pattern of tit for tat, of cost/benefit analysis in personal relationships. He calls us to his kind of love, a generous love that blesses evildoers. In the first of his five illustrations, Jesus says when you are insulted, turn the other cheek.

1. Insults

"Turn the other cheek" is more about insults than physical violence. Since most people were right handed, Jesus is talking about a backhand to the right cheek. In the world of that time, this was like spitting in someone's face. It was a great insult. Followers of Jesus do not worry about protecting our own honor. We bear insults without responding. This does not mean that we are to be doormats, fragile or weak. Rather, we are anvils. Not to respond when you are insulted is not weakness, but great strength. This is the meek person: the one who shows strength under control; an anvil that can take being hit by the hammer because it is stronger than the hammer.

How do you respond when another woman makes a cutting remark? "I've lost some weight. Do you want any of my old clothes?" Men, trash talk can get personal and cross a line when your manhood or mom gets dragged into it. More painful still are racial slurs, being called, "white trash," "wetback," or the N word. Jesus calls us to turn the other cheek. If you are in the majority culture, imagine being Hispanic or Black and having these slurs thrown at you. How would you respond? When he was insulted, Jesus turned his other cheek.

What does turning the other cheek mean for the wife whose husband is beating her? What about a victim of crime? Jesus is not saying that we are to let ourselves be abused. Jesus stands up for the oppressed. If you are being abused, get help. Call your church or the police. The point of this portion of the Sermon on the Mount is that we are to be concerned for the other person's good. We hold ourselves back from striking their cheek, from insulting them back. The next illustrations fill out the picture of what it means to bless evildoers. In the second illustration, Jesus says when faced with injustice, give your coat.

2. Injustice

Jesus describes a legal dispute in which a person is sued to take his shirt.

Matthew 5:40

And if anyone wants to sue you and take your shirt, hand over your coat as well.

The coat is an outer garment used to keep warm. You were not allowed by law to take someone's coat. Jesus paints a graphic illustration of what he means by nonresistance. Yet his point is not to give all your clothes away. It is unlikely that a lawsuit would be fought over a shirt. At stake is a deeper principle: even those things which we regard as ours by law, we must be prepared to abandon.[21] Jesus calls us to a radically unselfish attitude toward our rights and property. We should be more generous than the law requires. Years later, Jesus himself had his clothes taken away from him, even though he could have easily stopped that from happening.

In his famous novel *Les Misérables*, Victor Hugo tells the story of the Christlike Bishop Myriel who gives shelter to the main character Jean Valjean, an escaped prisoner. At night, Valjean runs off with Myriel's silverware. When the police capture Valjean, Myriel pretends that he has given the silverware to Valjean and presses him to take two silver candlesticks as well, as if he had forgotten to take them. The police accept his explanation and leave. Myriel tells Valjean that his life has been spared for God, and that he should use money from the silver candlesticks to make an honest man of himself. Myriel lived out Jesus' teaching. Frankly, I find Jesus' point extremely challenging, way above my current level of spiritual maturity. Of course, Jesus' next illustration is not any easier.

3. Imposition

When a person imposes on you, do more than they ask. "If someone forces you to go one mile, go with them two miles" (Matthew 5:41). Jesus is describing a situation common in his day. A Roman soldier had the legal right to conscript any Jewish person to carry his equipment for one Roman mile, defined as 1,000 paces. Jews who held to the letter of the law would walk exactly 1,000 paces and not a step more. Now Jesus comes along and says we are to volunteer to walk a second mile. We should not just submit to unjust impositions, but exceed them. Respond to oppression with kindness. The point is to go beyond the expected response, to do more than is asked.

The principle is that the requests of others come before my convenience.

I'm embarrassed to tell you how I failed at this. You see, one day I had my afternoon planned tightly: I would finish my work, go pick up a book at Half Price Books and arrive at LA Fitness just in time for racquetball. Tamara called and asked me to drive something my mom had left at our house over to my sister's house for her to take to my mom's. Welling up inside my head was an indignant "No" and thoughts such as: "Do you realize what I am doing? How busy I am? Why did my mom leave it anyway? My sister could come get it from my house." A little later I called Tamara back and sheepishly apologized. It's worse when you know my sister lives about five minutes from our house. In the end, I did take the stuff over and leave it at her door. Far from going the second mile, I was bucking at going the first few yards of the first mile. I have a long way to go. Pray for me.

Imagine if your roommate asks you to do the dishes and you not only do them but you clean the whole kitchen? What if your parent asks you to vacuum your room and you vacuum the whole house? What if your boss tells you to stay late and finish one piece of paperwork, but you stay even later and do his paperwork too? Jesus calls us to bless others by going beyond what's asked.

The fourth and fifth illustrations take us further into a positive direction. Jesus tells us to be generous to beggars and borrowers. Look at verse 42 where Jesus says if you get a request for money, give it.

Matthew 5:42

Give to the one who asks you, and do not turn away from the one who wants to borrow from you.

4. Request for money

Now you may be saying, "Wait a minute, Jesus. If I give money to everyone who asks me, pretty quickly I'm going to have no money. Then I'm going to have to start asking people for money. That makes no sense." What is Jesus' deeper point? We are to be generous. We are to be willing to share with people. We should not hold on to our money as if we need to protect it. Instead of protecting our money, we are to give it away freely to those who ask us, even to those who don't ask but we perceive to be in need.

This does not mean you give money to every professional beggar you encounter. It does not mean you fund every crazy business someone asks you to invest in. But those exceptions do not exempt us from giving money wisely and generously to people who ask for our help. How do you feel when someone asks for money from you? Does your stomach get tight? In your mind, do you immediately say, "No way"? Do you start thinking of ways to get out of it, reasons why you should not give any money? Jesus calls us to let go of a tightfisted attitude. Jesus' followers give generously as God gives to us.

What is your attitude toward your money? Do you see it as yours or as God's? Is it your money that you have to carefully protect or is it God's money that you must wisely steward? Jesus calls us to a generous heart that is willing to give without trying to figure out how we could benefit in return. In his illustrations, the overriding principle is that we are to bless people who do us wrong. We are to have a heart that is bigger than ourselves, less concerned about our hurts, and more concerned about other's needs. The final illustration of blessing evildoers has Jesus telling us that when someone expresses a desire to borrow something, we lend it.

5. Borrow something

How do you react inside when your neighbor wants to borrow your tools? Jesus is challenging our view of our possessions. Do they possess us or are they gifts from God to use for him? We should freely lend to those who want to borrow from us. Now, of course, as with all his illustrations, Jesus is not setting up a categorical rule, but pointing to deeper heart issues. You do not give all your stuff away until your house is empty to anyone who wants to borrow anything. But at a heart level, are you inclined first to lend or to hold back? What about loaning your brand new mower, or your favorite dress?

In all five illustrations, Jesus is saying self-sacrifice should replace self-protection. Blessing should replace retaliation. We are not trying to even the scales, but to bless others. We are putting their interests above our own. When we are wronged, our goal is not to get even, but to bless, to overwhelm them with unexpected kindness. We bake them cakes, send them flowers and mow their yard. We bless evildoers with no resistance. The second section of our passage supplements this first point. In Matthew 5:43–48, Jesus tells us to love your enemies: no hate.

6. Love your enemies

One more time, Jesus will counter "It was said" with "But I say to you." He calls us to divine love when he says:

Matthew 5:43–48

You have heard that it was said, "Love your neighbor and hate your enemy." But I tell you, love your enemies and pray for those who persecute you, that you may be children of your Father in heaven. He causes his sun to rise on the evil and the good, and sends rain on the righteous and the unrighteous. If you love those who love you, what reward will you get? Are not even the tax collectors doing that? And if you greet only your own people, what are you doing more than others? Do not even pagans do that? Be perfect, therefore, as your heavenly Father is perfect.

We all have enemies in our own minds. It is the politician you despise. It is your neighbor whose dog howls all night, who plays his music too loudly, who never returns the tools he borrows; the person who cuts you off on the freeway or humiliates you in public.[22] It's the boss who gives you a bad review, the company that fired you without cause, the person who lied about you behind your back and cost you the promotion, the person who blamed you for what they did wrong. It's the unfair teacher, it's the bully, it's the mean girls, or an ex-spouse. Sometimes it is a whole group of people you hate because someone from that group hurt you. Jesus' point is not just to withhold harm from our enemies, but to love them. This means we act in a loving way. Jesus is specific about one action. We are to pray for people who hurt us.

Pray for people who hurt you

Prayer expresses love and increases love. We pray for God to bless them. When you pray, bitterness dries up and anger fades. When you pray for them, your love grows. This week I read Harvard psychiatrist

Robert Coles' amazing account of counseling Ruby Bridges, who has become an iconic figure for racial harmony because of the Norman Rockwell painting now hanging in the White House.

In 1960 in New Orleans, six-year-old Ruby was to attend a white elementary school. All the white families pulled their children out of the school. Every teacher refused to teach, but one. Ruby went to school alone for an entire year. On her way to school and back from school, she was hounded by white activists screaming insults, slurs and even death threats to the point that she had to be escorted by U.S. Marshall Deputies. Because of his experience and education in child trauma, Coles volunteered to counsel her. He was astounded that she seemed fine. No nightmares. She drew no scary pictures. One day she told him that on her way to school, she prayed for those people in the crowd. Shocked, he asked why. She replied, "Don't you think they need praying for?" Coles confessed that in the same situation, that would not have been his response to the angry crowd. Ruby shared that her parents also prayed for the angry people and had taught her to pray for them.

How about you? Have you prayed for the person who hurt you? Have you put them on your prayer list? I challenge you to think of one person who has hurt you and commit to pray for them. Does someone come to mind, family member, boss, ex-spouse? If you are able to do it, I invite you to stop right now and pray a prayer of blessing for that person.

Prayer dries up bitterness, releases anger and increases love. To love our enemies, not only does Jesus call us to pray for people who hurt us, but also to greet people who are different from us.

Greet people who are different from you

If we only love those who love us and greet those who are like us, how do we stand out as different from worldly people? In the ancient world, a greeting was more than saying a quick "Hi." Greetings were bound up with blessings. Think about who you greet warmly. Do you avoid people of a different race, a different ethnicity, or a different religion? Jesus calls us to love people who are different from us by greeting them. Determine that you will go out of your way to greet people warmly who are different from you.

Jesus paints two kingdom pictures: to bless evildoers and to love our enemies. Why should we bless evildoers and love our enemies?

So you will be like your heavenly Father

In Jesus' kingdom vision, he calls us to imitate his father. We are to become people who model God's love. God is our father who blesses the evil and the good.

Who blesses

He brings sunshine and rain on all people, bringing life to the evil and the good. We are to be children of our Father in heaven, which means that we are to be like our divine dad. God loves and blesses people who hate him, who are opposed to him. We act like our divine dad when we love and pray for those who hurt us. Our heavenly Father is perfect.

Who is "perfect"

Jesus' last line in verse 48 gives the ultimate kicker: "Be perfect, therefore, as your heavenly Father is perfect." Essentially, Jesus is saying that we are to imitate the Father who is wholly good and totally loving. If we will follow Jesus' kingdom vision he has painted in Matthew 5, then we will be like our Father, loving all people in every way, even at great cost to ourselves. Jesus is summarizing the sermon so far: we should live a new kind of life, a God kind of life. This is the righteousness that surpasses that of the Jewish religious teachers. This is the good life, a Godlike life of love that he blesses.

But no human can do this. That is why Jesus had to come as our Savior. No human being could ever be righteous before God—except for Jesus, who lived a totally righteous life, died on the cross and rose again to deliver us from our sin while we were still against him. When you become a Christian, the Father sends the Holy Spirit to transform you from the inside out. Then your life can overflow with the love of Jesus. No one can live a perfect life on earth, but thankfully, we have a perfect Savior who provides a perfect salvation so that we stand perfect before God in Jesus.

As Jesus' follower, in the Spirit's power, how will you bless evildoers? How will you love an enemy? For whom will you pray blessings? Who will you go out of your way to warmly greet? If we will love our enemies and bless evildoers, we will be like our heavenly Father and we will shine a bright light in a dark world filled with revenge and hate. We will show people Jesus.

▌

For further study on chapter 4, see page 139.

CHAPTER FIVE

Your Kingdom Come

Matthew 6:1–18

If I am honest with myself, the truth is that I want you to think I am a spiritual guy; that I am good at giving, praying and fasting. After all, I'm a pastor, right? In quiet moments I ask myself, am I more concerned about the appearance of spirituality or the reality?

Of course, we should all be giving and praying, but with what motive? In Matthew 6, Jesus takes us beyond basic spiritual activities to our heart motives. At a core level, there is an audience question: Am I doing spiritual activities so other people will think I am spiritual, or am I doing them for my heavenly Father?

We are now right in the middle of the Sermon on the Mount in which Jesus presents his kingdom vision. His overall point is that we are to obey his authoritative teaching on the true meaning of the King's commands so that we might stand out as bright lights in the world, stand strong when storms come and step up to receive God's eternal reward. He calls us to be all in, people who hold nothing back as we follow him.

People misconstrue Christianity and what it means to follow Jesus because we humans are drawn to rules, to competition and fairness, meaning we get what we deserve. But the gospel of Jesus Christ does not operate that way. God calls us out of rules into a personal relationship with him as our Father; out of fairness into grace, getting what we don't deserve. Jesus' kingdom vision for spiritual activities, such as giving and praying, sees them not as meritorious acts that gain points with God, nor even as intrinsically good in themselves, but rather as ways to connect with our heavenly Father and all that relationship can entail. What if, rather than trying to earn God's favor or show other people how spiritual we are, we lived for God alone with ears listening for his "well done"? Jesus' big point is that his followers should aim to please God alone.

However, it's important to note that Jesus assumes we will give our money, pray to the Father and fast. In each of his three examples, he does not say IF you do these activities, but WHEN you do them. Many of us need to get to first base. We need to give because we don't. We need to pray more because we do too little of it. And we need to consider fasting. Then we can search our hearts for why we give, pray, or fast.

In our text, Jesus engrains a few central truths into our hearts by following a pattern in what he says about giving, praying and fasting. It starts with "*when you*" give to the needy, pray or fast. Then "*do not*" announce your giving like the hypocrites, pray like hypocrites or look somber when you fast like hypocrites. In each case, he addresses the intent that you will be seen by people. If that is your intent, then you will get only the reward of people's opinion of you and nothing from your heavenly Father. In contrast, you should do them without seeking an audience, give in secret, pray in a secret room and wash your face when you fast. Then in each case, the Father who sees what is done in secret will reward you. Our aim is to live for God alone, for his honor, not ours. Spiritual activities are not to be a display for others, but acts of devotion to our Father. Jesus summarizes his overall point:

Matthew 6:1

Be careful not to practice your righteousness in front of others to be seen by them. If you do, you will have no reward from your Father in heaven.

In those days, Jewish people would arrange to be in public places during the time for prayer so they could stop and pray where others would see them. What about us today? Today, a public place is the Internet through social media. On Facebook and Instagram, we can display our amazing vacations and incredible meals. We can also show how spiritual we are by posting about our time in God's Word, or the length of our fast. This is not to say that it is wrong to talk about Jesus on social media. We should, but with a heart to honor God, not to display our spirituality.

In fact, this verse seems to oppose what Jesus taught a few verses earlier when he said, "In the same way, let your light shine before others, that they may see your good deeds and glorify your Father in heaven" (Matthew 5:16). How can we reconcile these truths so that we do not do our righteousness in front of others and at the same time, we let our light shine? The key to resolving the conflict is in evaluating our heart motives. We are not to act spiritual in front of people so they will see how great we are, but rather we are to let our light shine so people will see how great God is. Our actions should point not to us but to Jesus. So by all means, talk about your relationship with God on social media but do it for the Lord, not for people to look at you.

In doing so we quickly substitute the great goal of pleasing God for the gross goal of pleasing people. Let's look at each of Jesus' three examples: giving, praying and fasting.

Give

Money is a sensitive topic. Jesus hits it head on.

Matthew 6:2–4

> *So when you give to the needy, do not announce it with trumpets, as the hypocrites do in the synagogues and on the streets, to be honored by others. Truly I tell you, they have received their reward in full. But when you give to the needy, do not let your left hand know what your right hand is doing, so that your giving may be in secret. Then your Father, who sees what is done in secret, will reward you.*

First, Jesus says what we are not to do. Once again, he uses a humorous, exaggerated illustration.

Don't blow a trumpet

We have a similar expression in English: Don't toot your own horn. He mentions "synagogues" and "streets" as public places where a person could be seen. How does this happen today? People want their name on a plaque or on a list of platinum sponsors. When you give so people will notice, Jesus says, truly you have received your reward in full. These are damning words using a commercial term that means you have been paid in full and so you will get nothing else. This implies that you will receive nothing from your heavenly Father; echoing back to verse 1, the Father will not reward you. In us there lurks a self-centered desire to be applauded for our spiritual deeds, but that desire blinds us to the real reward of a rich relationship with our Father.

Instead of blowing a trumpet, Jesus uses another hyperbole to share how we should give.

Left hand vs. right hand

Our left hand should not know what the right hand is doing. Taken literally, this would be impossible. What is Jesus saying? We should not display our giving so others know what we have given in the hopes they will think well of us. The point is about our motives. So is it wrong to give by check or online rather than with cash because then someone will know what we gave? Should you report charitable contributions on your taxes because then the Internal Revenue Service knows your giving? Should we only give in untraceable cash? No. Such external rules miss the point. The point is not external, but internal.

It is not necessarily wrong to have your name on a list of sponsors who give to a charitable event. It is not wrong for people to know how much you give. Jesus praised the widow who gave all she had and named the amount she gave. In the Book of Acts, clearly people knew that Barnabas had given a field at a certain price. Rather, the issue is your heart. The contrast is not public versus secret, but for God versus for show. However, most people find that keeping their giving private helps guard their heart from seeking people's approval. When you give not for people's praise, but to honor God, your Father rewards you.

Your Father will reward you

Rewards are a major theme in the Sermon on the Mount and in this section, the word "reward" is used seven times. For me, the concept of living to get rewards from God has felt awkward as if something is not quite right with it. Some have criticized Jesus, arguing that we should do good deeds altruistically with no thought of how we might benefit, even from God. While I sure do not want to criticize Jesus, the concept of rewards has been a bit weird for me. So I dug deeper into what the New Testament teaches about rewards. What I found has fascinated me and taken me to a deeper place with God.

You see, in Jesus' kingdom vision, rewards are not a commercial transaction, but a family connection. We are the Father's children. When your four-year-old son builds a tower out of blocks, you do not pay him a dollar. You delight in the tower and share the moment together. Our reward is the joy of the Father. To dip into ethical theory for a moment, this is deeper than doing what's in our best interest, deeper than doing what brings the most good, and even deeper than altruism, as if we do good because it is intrinsically good. Rather, the core reality is that God is God and the highest motive is to seek his good and share in it. The one who comes to God must believe this and that he rewards those who seek him (Hebrews 11:6). God does not give us rewards as a just judge based on our merits, but as a generous Father who graciously gives us far more than we could ever deserve.

Jesus rejects the entire thought of a moral calculus earning divine rewards, as if the rewards were monetary, or brownie points that we deserve. Rather, the Father's reward is his gracious offer for us to share in his triune divine life, to be adopted into his family and to participate in his eternal reign of peace. Jesus transcends religious notions of rewards as something a human merits by their actions. For him, rewards come from God's love and kindness in the gospel that offers us what we do not deserve. We do not give and pray so that we will get a cookie from God, but rather because we know that God is God and we want to please him.

Consider the example of a violin player. If you are a novice violin player, you can enjoy playing in a symphony, but not near the level of enjoyment that a master violinist experiences playing that same symphony. The master player's appreciation and enjoyment is so much richer. Then consider rewards from others. As a musician you feel good if a random person off the street claps for you when you play. But if the composer of the symphony is there when you play, and he smiles, that means everything to you. The more we mature in our life with Jesus, the more we experience God's reward now and in the future.

At a very deep level then, Jesus opens our hearts to see if we are doing spiritual actions, such as giving, for ourselves or for God himself.

So, how is your giving? This is an awkward question for many of us. Why is it difficult to ask each other this question? Jesus spoke right to the issue. He did not dodge it. You can't address motives for giving unless you are giving. In most churches, many people who attend do not give anything to the church. You might check into the reality of giving at your own church, and offer to be part of the solution. Giving leads to a truly God blessed life.

We have a spiritual challenge. Our giving is to be proportionate to how God has blessed us financially. God wants us to joyfully give. Talk with God about your giving. If you are giving zero, start giving something. Take a baby step. Start with ten dollars. If you are not proportionate in your giving, begin giving a percentage of your income. My prayer is that you will grow in this area of your spiritual maturity. Then we need to ask ourselves, what are my motives for giving? These same principles in regard to giving apply also to Jesus' second example: prayer.

Pray

In the Sermon on the Mount, Jesus takes more time on prayer than on either giving or fasting. He addresses two bad motives in prayer.

Matthew 6:5–8

And when you pray, do not be like the hypocrites, for they love to pray standing in the synagogues and on the street corners to be seen by others. Truly I tell you, they

> *have received their reward in full. But when you pray, go into your room, close the door and pray to your Father, who is unseen. Then your Father, who sees what is done in secret, will reward you. And when you pray, do not keep on babbling like pagans, for they think they will be heard because of their many words. Do not be like them, for your Father knows what you need before you ask him.*

Can you remember the first time you were asked to pray aloud? Your hands started sweating. Your mouth dried up. How did you start the prayer, "Dear God, Father, Lord, Jesus...?" You wondered if you should change the tone of your voice into a proper prayer tone: an octave lower than your normal voice. Is there a right way to pray? A right tone? A right vocabulary? Why do those questions even occur to us? To whom are we praying anyway? We should be praying to our Father, not for people to evaluate the quality of our piety. We should not pray to impress people, but to connect with God.

Motives

We do not pray so people will think we are spiritual. Sometimes with just a surface reading of the passage, people misunderstand Jesus. They think we should not pray in public, but only in secret. Jesus, however, is not talking about where we pray, but why we pray. Jesus prayed in public. The point is about what's inside our hearts, not the specific words that come out.

For instance, it is not wrong to pray before eating a burger in public at Chili's. The issue is not praying aloud at a restaurant, but why are you praying aloud? Is it to thank God for providing your daily food or is it so the people around you will think you are spiritual? We see someone across the restaurant who goes to our church, so we want to be sure they see us praying. The goal of connecting with our Father can be traded for its cheap distortion, the goal of impressing people.

Getting God to hear you

The second motive that can pollute our prayer is trying to get God to hear us so he will do what we wish him to do. The Father is not a reluctant listener. So we do not need to inform him of our needs or convince him to meet our needs. He knows us and he loves us. The issue is deeper than the length of our prayers or the exact words that we say in our prayers. There is no Christian prayer formula. Prayer is talking with our Father. Jesus prayed all night and prayed short prayers such as from the cross. He sometimes prayed a prayer once, and in the Garden of Gethsemane, he repeated his prayer. God is neither ignorant so that we need to instruct him, nor hesitant so that we need to convince him. Prayer is not twisting God's arm. We pray to connect with God and express our trust in him to meet our needs. Jesus says rather than praying in the street, we should go into our secret room.

Secret room

Jesus says we should pray in secret with the door closed. The room Jesus refers to would have been a small storage closet inside a single room home. As with giving, we can guard our heart by praying privately. So how is your prayer life? It's hard to talk about motives if you really don't pray much. To start with, you should pray a lot. When you pray in public, are you overly conscious of how others are hearing your prayer, or are you simply talking with your Father? When you pray to your Father, your Father will reward you.

God will reward you

When prayer is simply talking to the Father without worrying about what others think of us, we experience reward from the Father. That reward is intimacy with the Father himself.

Model prayer

Jesus breaks his pattern at this point by giving us a model for prayer, the famous Lord's Prayer, more appropriately called the disciple's prayer since it is intended for us. Jesus says:

Matthew 6:9–15

> *This, then, is how you should pray: "Our Father in heaven, hallowed be your name, your kingdom come, your will be done, on earth as it is in heaven. Give us today our daily bread. And forgive us our debts, as we also have forgiven our debtors. And lead us not into temptation, but deliver us from the evil one." For if you forgive other people when they sin against you, your heavenly Father will also forgive you. But if you do not forgive others their sins, your Father will not forgive your sins.*

When we say, "Our Father in heaven," we are not uttering a formal address, but celebrating a relationship.[23] We can only call God "Father" because of the high price he paid to adopt us as his children. When we are born, God is our Creator. We must be born again for God to be our Father. That only happens through Jesus Christ. The Bible says:

John 1:12

Yet to all who received him, to those who believed in his name, he gave the right to become children of God.

What an incredible privilege to be adopted into the family of God!

In this prayer, Jesus models six basic petitions in two groups of three. The first three focus on honoring God and the second three express our dependence on God.

Honor God

Most of us typically start by praying for our own needs. What can God do for me? Instead, Jesus instructs us that God Almighty should be our first concern. Seeking his honor puts requests for ourselves in proper perspective. This is not about a formula to follow every time we pray, but an attitude of our heart that puts God first.

Your name

The name of the Lord stands for God's character, nature, power, and authority. To honor God's name means to declare who he is. Our temptation is to try to make a name for ourselves rather than promoting his name.

Your kingdom

We anticipate the coming of our King in full power as we pray that Christ will exercise his revolutionary power today. "Your kingdom come" in my life, my family, my job, my city, my nation. We want his rule to be the rule of our lives.

Your will

Your will be done in me as it is in heaven. We are asking God to do what is necessary to make his will prevail in our lives and in our world, that God's desires for righteousness will be as fully accomplished *now* on earth as they are *now* in heaven. God's will be done in my marriage, my relationships and my career. Having expressed our burning concern for his glory, we now express our humble dependence on his grace.

Depend on God

Jesus models praying for daily bread, debts and deliverance.

Our daily bread

We are told to pray daily for bread, basic needs—not for daily cake and goodies for us. By asking for our daily bread, we are acknowledging that our lives are in God's hands. We recognize that all we have ultimately comes from the Lord.

Our debts

Forgiveness is as indispensable to the life and health of the soul as food is for the body. God's gracious forgiveness is based on what Jesus did on the cross, not on anything we do or don't do. Lack of forgiveness hurts our relationship with God. Thank God for his forgiveness.

Our deliverance

How could God ever lead us into temptation? Why would he try to get us to sin? That makes no sense. The Bible tells us in James 1:13 that God never tempts anyone. So what is Jesus saying? The answer is that Jesus is using a figure of speech called *litotes* that expresses something by negating the contrary. For example, "not a few" means "many." Lead us not into temptation" means keep us away from temptation. Lead us, *not* into temptation, but away from it, into righteousness. I encourage you to use Jesus' model not as a formula, but as a pattern for your prayer.

Fast

In the last three verses, Jesus moves to his third example, fasting. We will see the same pattern as we saw with prayer and giving:

> **Matthew 6:16–18**
>
> *When you fast, do not look somber as the hypocrites do, for they disfigure their faces to show others they are fasting. Truly I tell you, they have received their reward in full. But when you fast, put oil on your head and wash your face, so that it will not be obvious to others that you*

> *are fasting, but only to your Father, who is unseen; and your Father, who sees what is done in secret, will reward you.*

Fasting means to voluntarily abstain from food and, by extension, it has been used for voluntarily abstaining from activities such as television or social media. Fasting is never commanded in the Bible, but it is assumed by Jesus. So fasting is a voluntary spiritual practice. In the Bible, godly people fasted for repentance from sin, to ask God for wisdom in a crisis or a difficult decision, and to increase devotion in seeking God. When I fast, I tell myself that every time I feel a hunger pain, I will convert it to a spiritual hunger pain to know God more. As with giving and prayer, Jesus tells us not to fast so people will see us. He says, don't put on a sad face for show.

Don't put on a sad face for show

In Jesus' day, people would deliberately arrange their appearance to show they were fasting so people could see how devout they were. There is a word play in Greek. They made themselves unrecognizable to be recognized.[24]

Wash your face

Why would you tell other people you are fasting? There could be practical reasons. Since I do not do much of the cooking, I want Tamara to know not to cook dinner for me. But the real question is about my motive: am I sharing that I am fasting for people to see me? If you are medically able, I encourage you to try fasting for the right reasons.

Your Father will reward you

If you fast for the Father, your heavenly Father will reward you as he does with giving and praying. Our Father rewards us with the joy of nearness to him, with eternal blessings we cannot even imagine.

What is Jesus saying to us in this text? We should give, pray and fast, not for people but for God. We shouldn't give in order to impress others, we shouldn't pray to highlight our spirituality, and we shouldn't fast so that others are aware of our supposed humility. Spirituality is not a performance for people; it is faithfulness to a Person.[25] We should not give, pray and fast to impress others, but to connect with the Father. What is the Spirit of God saying to you in this passage? Engage in spiritual practices of giving, praying and fasting so you will connect more deeply with God and participate in what he is doing in the world. His reward is worth more than anything this world offers.

■

For further study on chapter 5, see page 147.

CHAPTER SIX

You Cannot Serve Two Masters

Matthew 6:19–34

Two issues are a big problem for American Christians. These issues are so huge that they strangle us. They restrict us from being all God has called us to be and do. These issues are like heavy chains around our necks. The chains are so thick that it will take the Spirit of God to break them. Jesus addresses both of them: money and worry.

Money and worry often go together. In Matthew 6:19–34, as he has throughout the Sermon on the Mount, Jesus calls us to single-minded devotion to him alone. We are to be all-in Christ followers, holding nothing back. In this text, we will see that we are to live for God alone, trusting him without worry. Jesus puts it to us in stark terms: Will we pursue God or money, the things of this earth or the priorities of Jesus Christ?

Money and worry strangle us, keeping us from serving God. Americans have fallen into the deadly trap of thinking that having more money and stuff will enhance our well-being, yet, study after study confirms that is not true. David G. Myers, author of "The American Paradox: Spiritual Hunger in an Age of Plenty," wrote in an American Psychologist article: "Our becoming much better off over the last four decades has not been accompanied by one iota of increased subjective well-being."[26] Over 2,000 years ago, Jesus shocked his audience with a similar message.

In the last chapter, we heard Jesus teach us to pray for God's kingdom to come and to pray for our daily bread. In the second half of Matthew 6, Jesus goes deeper into what it looks like to live for God's kingdom alone and how to trust God for our daily bread without worry. Could it be that by God's power we can become people who are not obsessed with material things, people who do not worry? What if we really did live for God alone, investing our best efforts and finances in his cause? It's a fundamental choice: living for the things of this earth or the things of God's kingdom.

Have you ever been to a Third World country? After coming back, it's common to feel guilty when we throw away the excess food on our plates or look at all the tee shirts in our closets. Then a few days later, we get over it and are back at the mall. Americans waste more money than most people around the world make in a lifetime. I ask you to be honest with yourself. To what extent have you become materialistic?

Live for God, Not Money

In verses 19–21, Jesus gives us three concrete illustrations to help us see that we have a fundamental choice to make. Jesus says:

Matthew 6:19–21

Do not store up for yourselves treasures on earth, where moths and vermin destroy, and where thieves

> *break in and steal. But store up for yourselves treasures in heaven, where moths and vermin do not destroy, and where thieves do not break in and steal. For where your treasure is, there your heart will be also.*

Treasure refers to what is precious to you. Jesus says we should have one heart: invest treasure in heaven, not earth.

One Heart

We should invest our treasure in heaven for two reasons: it lasts and our heart follows it. What does he mean to store up treasures on earth, and what does he not mean? Jesus is not forbidding owning private property, saving for retirement or buying life insurance.

It is not wrong to possess things, *but it is wrong for things to possess us.* It is wrong to be obsessed with stuff or to find our security in amassing money. Check your heart. Why do we keep buying bigger and better television sets, and the latest smart phones, or fashions? Ask yourself penetrating questions that can reveal your heart. Are you dreaming about making more and more money only to buy more and better stuff? Are you living beyond your means, racking up credit balances for stuff you buy? Are you giving very little to God's work? Do you rent a storage facility? How much is in it? When did you last look at what's there? Do we really understand that our true home is heaven and that is where we should be building our portfolio?

Suppose your home is in Switzerland and you're visiting America for two years, living in a Residence Inn. You're told that you can't bring anything back to Switzerland on your flight home. But you can earn money and send deposits to your bank in Switzerland. Would you fill your Residence Inn suite with expensive furniture and wall hangings? Of course not. You'd send your money where your home is. We're decorating hotel rooms! We know we can't take it with us. We know our true home is in heaven, but we are decorating hotel rooms! What are we doing?! Jesus says don't store up treasures on earth because only heavenly treasure lasts.

Only heavenly treasure lasts

Jobs vanish; banks disappear; huge companies go bankrupt. Retirement accounts disappear. Earthly treasures do not bring real security, just more to worry about. A treasure in heaven is anything we do on earth that will last for eternity. We store up treasure in heaven when we help other people find and follow Jesus Christ because people last forever.

Jesus is speaking specifically about money. We are to use our money on earth in such a way that we build up a balance in heaven. We invest in God's cause, in Christ's church. Give to the poor. Use the money God gives you to share and show the love of Jesus Christ. Why does Jesus say treasures in heaven are better than earthly treasures? Because there is no risk. Heavenly treasures are absolutely secure. Just on the level of making wise investments, there is no comparison between earthly and heavenly treasure.

A few years ago, I took my family to Austin, the home of The University of Texas (Hook 'em Horns!). After touring the state capital, we visited the gift shop where I bought reproductions of Republic of Texas currency. In 1836, the Republic of Texas coined money. Unfortunately, six years later, even the government wouldn't accept it for payment of taxes. Imagine you're living in the Republic of Texas in 1836. You've accumulated lots of Republic of Texas currency. You know that the currency will soon be worthless. Texas will join the Union and use the currency of the United States. What will you do with your Republic of Texas money? If you're smart, there's only one answer. You should immediately cash in your Republic of Texas currency for U. S. currency. Keep only enough Texas money to meet your short-term needs.

As a Christian, you have the ultimate insider trading tip: Earth's currency will soon become worthless. It only makes sense to invest in what will last. Your earthly money will be worthless in heaven, but you can use your money today to gain eternal treasure.

Your heart follows your money

Your heart goes where you put your money. In other words, you invest your money and your heart will follow. We know this from ordinary life. If you invest money in a stock, you are suddenly very interested in that company. You read articles on it. You follow it. Or if you put money into a fantasy football league, suddenly you are watching football games you never cared about before. You normally wouldn't even follow those teams, but they have a player on your fantasy team. Consider video games and your in-app purchases. When you buy coins for Clash of Clans, you are very interested in the game. If you want to have a heart for God and his kingdom, give your money to it. If you want your heart set on the priorities of our heavenly Father, then financially invest heavily in his cause. From the illustration of treasure, Jesus moves to vision.

One vision

Jesus' point is that we need one vision to see clearly what really matters. Here is what Jesus says:

Matthew 6:22–23

The eye is the lamp of the body. If your eyes are healthy, your whole body will be full of light. But if your eyes are unhealthy, your whole body will be full of darkness. If then the light within you is darkness, how great is that darkness!

The Greek word for "good" can mean singular and has a nuance of generous. Metaphorically, Jesus is saying that a good or generous eye, focused on God, will give us clear mental focus. However, a bad or stingy, envious eye will distort our vision. Jesus says you cannot look in two directions at the same time. We should focus our vision on the good things of the kingdom.

Bright life vs. dark life

When we get focused on earthly stuff rather than heavenly treasure, our whole perspective gets distorted. If our vision becomes clouded by the false god of materialism, then our whole life is in darkness and we cannot see where we are going. We get confused about what's important. We become spiritually disoriented. Jesus is saying our generosity, or lack of it, is a significant indicator of our spiritual maturity. From treasures and vision, one heart and one vision, Jesus takes us to the deepest level.

One master

Jesus says:

Matthew 6:24

No one can serve two masters. Either you will hate the one and love the other, or you will be devoted to the one and despise the other. You cannot serve both God and money.

Jesus boldly declares that you cannot serve two masters. The reason you must serve God and not money is simply because you cannot serve both.

You Cannot Serve Both

Many people argue with Jesus on this point. I have. Can't I be a godly person and make lots of money? Of course you can. But the fact that we ask the question may betray a heart issue inside. Remember in the Sermon, Jesus is not focused on external behavior, but on heart level issues. Materialism may be the single biggest competitor today for the hearts of Christian people. Jesus says take your pick: God or money, but you can only pick one.

Jesus' point is not that is it unspiritual to serve God and money, but that it is impossible. You either serve God or money. Jesus says either we will hate the one and love the other or be devoted to one and despise the other. This sounds absolute. In Hebrew thought, love and hate refer to allegiance. There can only be one Number One. The point is not about emotions, but allegiance. When a man marries his wife, it doesn't necessarily mean that he hates the women he didn't marry. It does mean that he should end any emotional relationships with other women. He does not share his marriage with other women emotionally. Are you trying to share God with money?

Here are some questions to test who you really serve. Have you ever explained that you do not serve in your church because you have to work so much? What percentage of your assets would you be willing to liquidate to finance a ministry project that promoted Jesus' kingdom?[27] Does God only get your spare change? What percent of your income do you give to God? We break the power of materialism by generous and cheerful giving.[28]

If we are not giving any money to our local church, then we are not trusting and honoring God with our money. If we are not giving proportionately as God has blessed us, then we are not being faithful.

We are not mature in this area of life. By and large that means that we are not investing our treasures in heaven, but on earth. We have a heart problem. We can experience a more joyous, blessed life if, by faith, we will start giving something on a regular basis and see what God does in our heart. Watch how it affects your relationship with your heavenly Father. I want you to have a blessed life. It comes through obeying Jesus Christ.

Jesus calls us to choose: we cannot store up treasure in two places. We cannot look in two directions at once or serve two masters. Jesus wants no rivals. Where are you storing up treasures? Where are your eyes focused? Who is your master? If you live for God, then you do not have to worry.

Trust God, Don't Worry

If you displace God with money, you will be consumed with worry, but if you trust God with your needs, you can be free from worry. Some call this next section our Savior's stress test.[29] The extent of your worry reveals the lack of your faith. Verse 25 starts with the word "therefore" linking the section on money with the next section on worry. Worry strangles our ability to serve God. Imagine if you could live free from anxiety. Jesus says:

Matthew 6:25–32

Therefore I tell you, do not worry about your life, what you will eat or drink; or about your body, what you will wear. Is not life more than food, and the body more than clothes? Look at the birds of the air; they do not sow or reap or store away in barns, and yet your heavenly Father feeds them. Are you not much more valuable than they? Can any one of you by worrying add a single hour to your life? And why do you worry about clothes? See

> *how the flowers of the field grow. They do not labor or spin. Yet I tell you that not even Solomon in all his splendor was dressed like one of these. If that is how God clothes the grass of the field, which is here today and tomorrow is thrown into the fire, will he not much more clothe you—you of little faith? So do not worry, saying, "What shall we eat?" or "What shall we drink?" or "What shall we wear?" For the pagans run after all these things, and your heavenly Father knows that you need them.*

The point is clear. It is not hard to understand. It's doing it that is hard. It boils down to faith. Do you trust God? Tamara told me I could share that she struggles with worry so this is one of her favorite passages in the Bible. Worry affects Tamara physically with muscle aches and lack of sleep. We call her tense muscles her sin meter. When her body is reacting that way, she knows she is not trusting God. Jesus gives seven compelling reasons why we do not need to worry.

1. Life is more important than stuff

Life is about more than eating. Jesus says do not worry about your physical needs because life is more than that and if God gave you life, surely he will feed and clothe you.

2. Your Father will feed you

Birds do not worry about their food. They do not sow seeds or store food in barns. And yet the Creator feeds them. You are made in God's image, much more valuable than a bird. Certainly, God will feed you.

3. Worry is impotent

Worry does not help. "Who of you by worrying can add a single hour to his life?" (Matthew 6:27). To worry about what we can't help is useless; to worry about what we can help is needless because we can act to correct the problem. Worry is like a rocking chair. It will give you something to do, but it won't get you anywhere. Essentially, worry is futile because it is powerless. Not only will it not help, it actually hurts. So why would anyone ever worry when it does no good?

4. God will clothe you

Flowers do not labor for their beautiful color. If the Creator clothes flowers that are very temporary, will he not clothe his children who are eternal? Even Solomon, the great King of Israel who was renowned for his enormous wealth, was not dressed as spectacularly as fields of wild flowers.

5. Worry is faithless

Jesus asks, "Will he not much more clothe you—you of little faith?" To worry about your food or clothes is to have missed the faith lesson from the birds and the flowers. God will feed you. God will clothe you. Worry reveals a lack of faith. If you have big worries, then you have a small god. Faith kills worry. Kingdom people are different. Jesus' followers do not need to worry.

6. Worry is pagan

"For the pagans run after all these things" (Matthew 6:32). The phrase "run after" is the same word used for "seek" in verse 33. Non-Christian people often focus their concern on earthly physical needs. The poor and the rich are both consumed with material worries, whether that is getting money or keeping money. It is pagan to be sinfully anxious. It's not the first emotion of anxiety that is the problem, it is indulging that feeling by stoking the emotional fire into sinful worry. Worry is a practical atheism that denies the existence of a good God who takes care of his children; in practice we are acting like God does not actively care for us. If we worry as much as our neighbors do, we are no different. It's our lack of worry that will set us apart.

7. Your Father knows your needs

We should be different from the people around us because we trust that our heavenly Father knows our needs. Do you trust God for your physical needs? Jesus says we do not have to worry for seven solid reasons: life is more important than stuff; your Father will feed you more than the birds; worry is impotent; God will clothe you more than the flowers; worry is faithless; worry is pagan; and finally, your Father knows your needs. It boils down to trust. Do you trust God? Then don't worry. Jesus summarizes both parts of the passage in the last two verses.

Seek first God's righteous rule without worry

It's fascinating to me that the opposite of worrying about our needs is not taking a nap or resting in the recliner, but proactive action for something else: Jesus' kingdom. Jesus says:

Matthew 6:33–34

But ***seek*** *first his kingdom and his righteousness, and all these things will be given to you as well. Therefore do not worry about tomorrow, for tomorrow will worry about itself. Each day has enough trouble of its own.*

Jesus directs our attention away from worrying about earthly needs to focusing on his kingdom rule. "Seek" is a present imperative implying an unceasing quest. We are to focus our energies on Jesus' kingdom rule. In the right sense, we are to "worry" about God's mission. To what extent are we helping people find and follow Christ? Are we investing our resources in that mission? What do you "seek first"? When Jesus' followers seek his kingdom first, God will provide for them.

God will provide for you

Does this mean that no Christian will ever die of hunger? No. Jesus intended these statements as a general rule. The overwhelming importance of the kingdom may require self-sacrifice, even to the ultimate degree. Jesus himself died on the cross. Believers are not exempt from trouble, but from worry. Jesus ends the chapter with another wise saying.

Today is enough

This should be common sense, but living this truth is anything but common. We never live in tomorrow. We only have today. Worrying about tomorrow does not help either tomorrow or today. If anything, it robs us of our effectiveness today—which means we will be even less effective tomorrow. Worry does not take the sorrow out of tomorrow, just (to be cheesy) the "yea" out of "today." When we worry about tomorrow, we misuse the strength God has provided for today. I love the line in the old song: "Many things about tomorrow I don't seem to understand. But I know who holds tomorrow and I know who holds my hand."[30]

Life is so much more than eating, drinking and clothing. These are what we see on magazine covers in the grocery story: drinking, eating and clothing, stuff of this earth. But we are engaged in God's worldwide mission. Worry is unnecessary, unproductive and unworthy of a follower of Jesus Christ. It betrays that we are not seeking Jesus' kingdom first. Who are you serving: God or money? Take a look at where you are storing your treasures. Where is your heart? Have the courage to face your own materialism, the courage to address your giving. Take action to stop worrying about something that normally gives you anxiety. Invest your money in Christ's kingdom mission to help people find and follow Christ. Seek first his kingdom!

▌

For further study on chapter 6, see page 157.

CHAPTER SEVEN

Do Not Judge

Matthew 7:1–12

Over 2,000 years ago, Jesus Christ taught at least two ethical principles that have become justifiably famous. Today these two are among the most well-known and repeated ethical principles, embraced by most people regardless of whether they are Christian or not.

The principles are "Do not judge" and the Golden Rule: "Do unto others as you would have them do unto you." But do we really understand what Jesus meant? These principles have been greatly misused and abused, and even ignored. Let's unpack Jesus' principles, asking how we can follow them faithfully today.

Matthew 7 opens with one of the most misused phrases Jesus ever spoke: "Do not judge." It has been used to justify utter relativism (i.e., the claim that there is no absolute truth). And it has been used to counter anyone who disagrees with your opinion: "Don't judge me." If I don't not like what you are saying, I can just accuse you of being judgmental, as if that stops all rational debate. Sadly, Christians today are widely perceived to be judgmental, full of hypocritical judgments, as if we are Maude Flanders from the Simpsons television show.

While we can write off these judgments against us as overblown, it is wiser for us to consider the measure of truth in the accusations. Christians have been judgmental. Some from our camp have painted hate-filled signs and paraded them in public. I'm embarrassed by some comments Christians put on social media. One of the greatest hindrances to the gospel of Jesus today is intolerant, judgmental Christians. When I ask people in a church if you feel you have ever been judged by another Christian, the majority raise their hand. You probably have. It is a problem. We need to start with looking at our own hearts.

What if rather than being known as judgmental, Christians were known as caring? What if we were people who always treated other people as we want to be treated ourselves? That's how Jesus calls us to live.

Do not hypocritically condemn others

The command "Do not judge" can be rephrased "Do not hypocritically condemn." Stay with me as I defend this interpretation. Jesus backs up his command "Do not judge" with a funny image from his carpentry shop. Imagine a person with a plank stuck in their eye. Jesus says:

Matthew 7:1–5

Do not judge, or you too will be judged. For in the same way you judge others, you will be judged, and with the measure you use, it will be measured to you. Why do you look at the speck of sawdust in your brother's eye and pay no attention to the plank in your own eye? How can you say to your brother, "Let me take the speck out of your eye," when all the time there is a plank in your

> *own eye? You hypocrite, first take the plank out of your own eye, and then you will see clearly to remove the speck from your brother's eye.*

Let's dive into the issue of what it means to judge. It does not mean we are to suspend our critical faculties. We know this because later in this chapter Jesus tells us to distinguish true from false prophets by examining their fruit. Paul says in 1 Corinthians 2:15, "The spiritual man makes judgments about all things." At first glance, it looks like the Bible contradicts itself. What does God want us to do? Are we supposed to judge or not?

From the vivid illustration of the plank and the speck, the context here argues that the verse means "Do not condemn." Do not adopt a critical spirit, a condemning attitude. We should make valid judgments between right and wrong, but we should not be judgmental. Jesus is not telling us to be blind, but gracious. We are to be discerning, but not condemning.

Too often we play God. We judge others without even really knowing all the facts. We are not to usurp the role of God who is the only true judge, the only one who knows the total situation. We are not God. In short, Jesus is saying, give up a critical, intolerant, rigid, petty, judgmental spirit that finds fault in everyone but yourself.

Jesus is not picturing a society of blind tolerance or moral indifference. If we never judge anything as true or false, good or evil, then we can make no moral distinctions: cannibalism becomes just another diet; marriage with multiple wives becomes another lifestyle, and terrorists become patriots. On a much milder level, we must not take Jesus to ridiculous extremes: Is Jesus saying it's wrong to judge a cake baking contest? Is it unchristian to declare a runner safe on first base? Is it unbiblical to call a foul in basketball? Are employers wrong to give their employees job reviews?[31] Of course not.

The point is that we are not to be faultfinders, condemning others, putting the worst interpretation on their motives, curious about their sins. We should not blindly judge others while we turn a blind eye to our failings.

It's so easy to put other people down, often behind their back. Somehow, in a twisted way, we make ourselves feel better when we pull others down. It makes us feel better to gloat over the sins and errors of others; hence our love of scandals. We distract ourselves with other people's drama, even with people we do not know personally, so we don't have to deal with our own drama. We lap up all the sordid details and every speck we collect helps us ignore the logjam in our own eye.[32]

Within church circles this takes bizarre forms: judging the spirituality of a young couple by observing whether they feed their baby on demand or on a schedule, judging others by the Bible version they use or by whether they drink a beer or wear yoga pants. Mommies can be the worst. Mommies war over bottle feeding vs. breastfeeding; stay-at-home moms vs. working moms; and front packs over slings.

We also judge people for watching R-rated movies, and whether they let their kids play first person shooter video games. Christians divide over their political affiliation as Republican, Democrat or something else. When our five kids were little, we got the wonderful question in the grocery store as people looked at the seven of us, "Don't you know what causes that?" Thanks a lot. Jesus does more than tell us not to hypocritically condemn others. He explains why it is a really bad idea. God will condemn you the same way.

You will be condemned in the same way

Jesus says that in the same way you judge others, you will be judged. The measure you use will be the one God uses to measure you. Sometimes Jesus motivates us with love and other times with consequences. The fear of God's judgment should motivate you to quit condemning other people. If we do not want God to judge us the way we are judging people, then quit it. Could you even imagine praying, "God condemn me as I judge others"? Next time you sit around talking down other people, picture God in heaven turning the conversation to you. It scares me to think about God judging me the way I have condemned other people, especially in my own home, often under the guise of humor. I hope it scares me straight so I don't condemn people anymore. Neither the privacy of a small circle of friends nor the guise of humor excuses judging others. We've heard from Jesus what we are not to do, but Jesus says more than do not hypocritically condemn.

Humbly help others

We are to help our brother get the speck out of his or her eye. But first we are to get the plank out of our own eye. A curious feature of our human race is a profound ignorance of our own faults combined with an arrogant presumption about others' faults. We're walking around with planks in our eyes inspecting our brother's and sister's eyes for specks of dust. How crazy! It is so easy for us to criticize in others what we excuse in ourselves. Many of us hold others to a much higher standard than we hold ourselves. We have a tendency to exaggerate the faults of others and minimize the gravity of our own.[33]

Remove the plank

Jesus says our first step is to remove the plank from our own eye. The Greek word, *dokos*, translated as "plank" refers to a massive timber beam used to support a roof. We can only judge others after we have judged ourselves. Have you had the painful experience of vividly seeing your own sin and then experiencing the amazing grace of God? That experience delivers you from a critical, judgmental attitude. How can we correct anyone else if we have not first corrected ourselves? If you are in conflict with another person, before you attack them for all they have done wrong, have you owned up to your part in the issue?

Rather than spending so much time complaining about the sin in the world, we should spend some time addressing the sin in our own lives. We tend to magnify others' sins and minimize ours. Projection is an all too common psychological reality. We project on others the very issue we are wrestling with. Because of his own guilt, a businessman, convicted of embezzling thousands of dollars, resembles a mother bear guarding her cubs when it comes to the petty cash box—everyone in the organization has to account for every dollar. A preacher has an affair with a woman in his church. The story makes national news because he campaigned against sexually-explicit magazines in 7-Eleven stores.[34]

We see and condemn in others what we hate in ourselves, but refuse to face. If you want to do something about sin in our society, start with yourself. We need to have the courage to do a probing moral inventory of ourselves. Then, and only then, with a clear view of our sin and an appreciation for the grace of God, can we see the speck in our brother's eye and be ready to humbly help. After we have removed the plank from our own eye, then Jesus says we are to remove the speck from our brother's eye.

Remove the speck

Echoing Jesus, Paul says in Galatians that if someone is caught in a sin, those who are spiritual should restore him gently (Galatians 6:1). Rather than condemning, we are to be caring. Rather than judging, we are to be helping. Abraham Lincoln wisely said: "He has the right to criticize who has the heart to help." Rather than turning a blind eye to sin, we are to help our brother get the speck out of his eye. I love the Marines' slogan: "No man left behind." When a fellow Christian falls into sin, we pick him up and help him heal.

Our help comes humbly with the realization that tomorrow we may need that person to help take a speck out of our eye, because we cannot see it! By definition, we can't see our blind spots.

Think about how you remove a splinter from another person's eye. We remove splinters gently. The eye is one of the most sensitive parts of our body. When you get your finger close to it, it closes. Some people cannot wear contact lenses because they could never put them in their eyes. To remove a speck from someone's eye, that person needs to trust you and you must be incredibly gentle. It's a very personal act.

Jesus is calling us to a high standard. Rather than being harsh judges condemning others, or hypocrites who blame others while excusing ourselves, we are to be loving friends who first deal with our own issues and then humbly and gently help our brother. Commenting on this text, British scholar John Stott said, "We need to be as critical of ourselves as we often are of others, and as generous to others as we always are to ourselves."[35] In a sense, this is an application of the Golden Rule, which we find at the end of our passage.

We are reminded again that Jesus did not prohibit all evaluation because in verse 6 he tells us to make a judgment about people. Jesus says humbly help others while avoiding those who do not want your help, because they will hurt you.

Avoiding those who don't want help

Culturally, back then, pigs were not like Wilbur from *Charlotte's Web*, but more like dangerous wild boars. And dogs were not anything like my amazing chocolate Labrador Retriever, Calvin. Rather, Jesus is referring to packs of wild scavenger dogs like you find in a third world city. Jesus says:

Matthew 7:6

Do not give dogs what is sacred; do not throw your pearls to pigs. If you do, they may trample them under their feet, and turn and tear you to pieces.

Jesus uses dogs and pigs to represent people who do not want your help. Jesus warns his followers against naïveté. Some people are closed and hostile. Jesus echoes proverbs such as:

Proverbs 9:7–8

Whoever corrects a mocker invites insults; whoever rebukes the wicked incurs abuse. Do not rebuke mockers or they will hate you; rebuke the wise and they will love you.

Some Christians in their well-meaning zeal can try to force an issue with a person who is mocking them. It is worthless and even dangerous to correct someone who is not willing to hear it. Until a person wants help, it does no good to give it. We need to learn when to walk away, when to be quiet and say nothing. Sometimes silence is the wisest response. How do we discern whether a person is a receptive brother or a dangerous dog? We need wisdom from God. So in verse 7, Jesus tells us to seek God for necessary wisdom.

Seek God

Jesus uses the words *ask, seek* and *knock*. He encourages us to seek God.

Matthew 7:7–11

Ask and it will be given to you; seek and you will find; knock and the door will be opened to you. For everyone who asks receives; the one who seeks finds; and to the one who knocks, the door will be opened. Which of you, if your son asks for bread, will give him a stone? Or if he asks for a fish, will give him a snake? If you, then, though you are evil, know how to give good gifts to your children, how much more will your Father in heaven give good gifts to those who ask him!

What causes you to hesitate to pray? Do you think your concerns are too small? That God has bigger things to worry about than your business or your kid's schoolwork? Do you doubt that God really answers prayer? Jesus' big point is that we should keep seeking God because our Father will respond. God is good. He wants to give us good gifts. Do we really believe that he is good or do we suspect he might trick us with a snake or a stone?

If you have trusted in Jesus Christ as your Savior, then God is your Father. You are his child. Jesus says to seek God because he will give you what you ask for, you will find what you seek and the door will be opened.

Prayer is like a child coming to their loving parent. We want our kids to talk to us about what's bothering them. I wonder if our heavenly Father is sad that we don't talk with him more often. But of course, not all that we ask for is given to us, and that is a good thing, because we don't always ask for beneficial things.

Only an irresponsible parent would give their child everything they asked for. No responsible parent gives their three-year-old a sharp knife even if he begs for it. We don't give our second grader a large bag of marshmallows for lunch. In fact, if I knew that God would give me everything I asked for, I would be afraid to pray for fear that I would ask for something that would really hurt me or hurt Christ's cause.

As a wise Christ follower once said:

> "I asked for strength that I might achieve; he made me weak that I might obey. I asked for health that I might do great things; he gave me grace that I might do better things. I asked for riches that I might be happy; he did not give them so that I might be wise. I asked for power that I might have the praise of men; I was given weakness that I might feel a need of God. I asked for all things that I might enjoy life. I was given life that I might enjoy all things. I received very few of the things that I asked for; but I received the things that I had hoped for."[36]

You can confidently keep on seeking God because he will give you good gifts. In context, God will us the good gift of wisdom in order to know how to see ourselves correctly, and others clearly, so we can take planks out of our own eye and specks out of our brother's eye.

Jesus brings this part of the sermon to a close with what has classically been called the Golden Rule. Look back to 5:17 where Jesus says that he fulfills the law and the prophets. Matthew 7:12 echoes that verse as Jesus says that this golden principle sums up the law and the prophets. I believe this is also what we are to ask the Father in prayer.

Do good to others

We seek the Lord to discover how to best do good to others. Many people have humorously distorted the Golden Rule. "He who has the gold makes the rules." "Do unto others what they have done unto you."

Or, "Do unto others before they do unto you." Jesus gives the true Golden Rule:

Matthew 7:12

So in everything, do to others what you would have them do to you, for this sums up the Law and the Prophets.

Jesus cuts to the heart of self-centeredness that obstructs us from obeying him. His rule is another way of saying that love is the summary of the law. As Jesus will say later, the whole law is summarized in loving God with all your heart and your neighbor as yourself. As Jesus' followers, we should love above all else. If we will love others, we will do for them what we would want done to us in the same circumstance. We will not condemn others, but humbly help them with gentle love. With the Father's good gifts, we do good to others.

How could you live out the Golden Rule? Start by thinking of the people closest to you. Put yourself in their shoes. What would you want, and then give it to them. Consider your relationships at work. Work is one of the most powerful places to love others with the Golden Rule. What would you want if you were one of your customers? If you were your boss? If you were a co-worker? If you were a supplier, a competitor?

Seriously pondering all of our relationships through the lens of Jesus' Golden Rule is challenging. It summons us to a divine kind of love that we can only exercise in the power of the Spirit. This is what it looks like to live in Jesus' kingdom vision. We are people who do not condemn others, but honestly address our own issues. Only then do we humbly help others with their issues. We seek God for wisdom in how to help them as we would want to be helped if it were a speck in our own eye.

Who can you stop judging? What plank can you remove from your eye? Who could you humbly help? How will you exercise the Golden Rule? We have a good Father who gives us the power and wisdom to seek first his kingdom, if we seek him in prayer. In the next chapter, we find the challenging conclusion to Jesus' sermon.

▌

For further study on chapter 7, see page 165.

CHAPTER EIGHT

Enter the Narrow Gate

Matthew 7:13–29

We come to Jesus' final challenge in the conclusion to his amazing Sermon on the Mount, the most famous and influential speech in history. Jesus started his address with blessings and ends it with warnings. He calls us to decision, to make a choice.

Jesus' overall point in the Sermon on the Mount is that we are to obey his authoritative teaching so that we might stand out as bright lights in this dark world, stand strong when storms come and step up to receive God's eternal reward. He calls us to be all in, people who hold nothing back. If we do, we will never be the same.

At the end of the sermon, he says there are only two choices: either follow him all in, holding nothing back, or not at all. Either give it your all or get off the field. Jesus describes three pairs of choices: two roads, two trees, and two houses. There are only two choices, not three or four. One leads to life and the other to destruction. Your choice determines your destiny. Which will you take?

To be faithful to Jesus' message, we should call ourselves to decision. So, let's be honest with ourselves in terms of where we are with Jesus. Each person is in a different place. Some are not sure what to think about Jesus. You may believe Jesus is a great man, but are not sure he is the resurrected Savior of the world. You may be among the many who at some time in your life said a prayer of salvation, were baptized or went through confirmation. But you have not seriously followed Jesus with full devotion. Or you may be among others who come to church regularly, serve and give some money, but in your heart you are not devoted to Jesus. You may be all in, holding nothing back. Jesus means everything to you and your life shows it. Jesus' words today are aimed mostly at those in the middle. Let me be frank because Jesus is. You need to make a decision. Can you imagine deciding to commit your life to follow Jesus with no reservations? If we would follow Jesus all in, holding nothing back, we would make a huge difference in our communities. What will you choose?

The key word in Jesus' conclusion is the Greek verb *poiein*, "to do" or "to practice," which occurs nine times in these last verses. For the sake of English style, translators use several words, including "do," "practice" and "perform." Repetition makes the point. Action is what counts. Just do it. Will you obey Jesus or are you just going through the motions? Are you affirming that Jesus is a great guy—but not your Lord, so you can go on living however you want to live?

Wherever you are with God right now, Jesus challenges us to decide to follow him without reservation, without qualification. At the end of the chapter, I will echo Jesus by calling you to decide. Let's take a look at the first of Jesus' three pairs, the two roads. His point is to take the narrow road because the wide road leads to destruction, but the narrow road leads to life.

Two Roads

Jesus says:

Matthew 7:13–14

Enter through the narrow gate. For wide is the gate and broad is the road that leads to destruction, and many enter through it. But small is the gate and narrow the road that leads to life, and only a few find it.

There is one simple command: "Enter the narrow gate." Wide is the road that leads to destruction. This is the more popular way. Here is the road for the majority. Generally, this is the road you follow if you want to follow the crowd. If you want to be popular in this life, this is the better road for you. It is a wide road that offers lots of options to do pretty much anything you want. You can be in charge of your life. There is total freedom, no boundaries. You do not have to give up anything. There's just one problem: this road is the highway to hell. The wide, popular road will destroy you in the end, and it may destroy you much sooner. People say there are many roads to God. Not true. There is one road to God. But there is a wide road to hell with lots of options for how to destroy yourself.

Jesus says small is the gate and narrow is the road that leads to life and only a few find it. The Greek word for "narrow" implies difficult. A few years ago, my wife Tamara and I vacationed in Colorado. Since I love the mountains, I wanted to get to the top of 14,130-foot Mount Evans. It has one road to the top, the highest paved road in America. Colorado Highway 5 is narrow and winding with steep drop-offs. But it is the only road to the summit. Tamara and I were driving on wide, smooth Interstate 70 headed to Denver. If we had stayed on Interstate 70, the driving would have been easy. We could have put on cruise control, but we would never have made it to our destination. To get to Mount Evans, we took the narrow winding

Highway 5 that suffers from falling rocks and hairpin turns. It was really hard driving, but we made it to the top.

If you want to make it to heaven, there is only one road that gets you there. It is called Jesus Christ. Jesus is the road to life. There is no promise that it will be an easy road. Here's the question: Are you more concerned about finding the easiest road or about where the road is taking you? Everything hinges on Jesus.

How do you respond to the word "narrow"? These days being narrow is a bad thing. I don't think of myself as narrow. Narrow people are small-thinking, bigoted people who put down others. They have not seen the world or read widely. But truth is narrow. There is one road to the top of Mount Evans. You can drive on lots of other roads in Colorado, but none of them will take you to the summit of Mount Evans. Truth by its very nature is narrow.

God provides salvation for everyone. Jesus is not exclusive, but inclusive. God loves the whole world and invites whoever will to be saved. People who follow Jesus are not narrow in who they love; they are called to love even their enemies. People who follow Jesus do for *all* others what they would want others to do for them.

Following Jesus leads to a destination far better than Mount Evans. It leads to life, full life, eternal life. Life is the experience of a personal relationship with God himself, the author of life. Take the narrow road and you will experience a full life on earth and then will arrive joyously in the heavenly kingdom. You have a choice to make: the wide road or the narrow road. Look at the different destinations. Jesus does not mince words. The wide road leads to destruction. That means destruction in this life and eternally. The wide road that promises so much freedom and fun will end in destruction. The narrow road leads to life. It is the best life.

Many voices tell you the broad road is better, that you don't have to take the narrow road. Some of those voices even come from religious people who will lead you the wrong way. How can you recognize false religious teachers?

Two Trees

Jesus shifts his image from roads to trees. Then he takes us to judgment day in, frankly, a terrifying scene. Listen to Jesus, starting in verse 15:

Matthew 7:15–23

Watch out for false prophets. They come to you in sheep's clothing, but inwardly they are ferocious wolves. By their fruit you will recognize them. Do people pick grapes from thornbushes, or figs from thistles? Likewise, every good tree bears good fruit, but a bad tree bears bad fruit. A good tree cannot bear bad fruit, and a bad tree cannot bear good fruit. Every tree that does not bear good fruit is cut down and thrown into the fire. Thus, by their fruit you will recognize them.

Not everyone who says to me, "Lord, Lord," will enter the kingdom of heaven, but only the one who does the will of my Father who is in heaven. Many will say to me on that day, "Lord, Lord, did we not prophesy in your name and in your name drive out demons and in your name perform many miracles?" Then I will tell them plainly, "I never knew you. Away from me, you evildoers!"

So how do we recognize false teachers? They may have a religious title such as pastor or bishop. They may use religious language. It's hard to spot religious counterfeits ("wolves") because they are disguised as sheep. Jesus gives one clear instruction: by their fruit you will recognize them. All is not as it appears. In the last chapter, we learned that we are not to be judgmental, but we are to be discerning. Jesus wants us to use our minds to distinguish true from false religious professionals. There are people who use religion to deceive people, to take their money. The way to distinguish the charlatans from the genuine is to check their fruit. Fruit is more than just the size of a ministry, it is who people really are, their character.

Please listen to Jesus because with the Internet, we now are exposed to more false religious teachers than ever in history. Do not let yourself be deceived. Check how their lives measure up to Jesus' sermon. What are their lives like? We are not looking for perfection, but at character and reputation, a pattern of life.

Sadly, we have too many examples of public scandals where a so-called Christian leader was exposed for sexual or financial sin. As you listen to religious teachers, look at their lifestyle. Are they making excessive money off people? Compare what a person is teaching with what Jesus has to say. Are they talking more about self-image, self-help, success, making money, and winning, or are they talking more about following Jesus no matter what the cost? Are they talking about sin and repentance? Know your Bible to compare their teaching to the Word of God. I invite you to check my life. You will find I am far from perfect, but with all my heart I aim to teach the Word of God without compromise and to obey the Word of God without qualification.

Very sadly, the self-delusion of false teachers will be exposed on judgment day. The scene in verses 21–23 is terrifying. Jesus declares that not everyone who says "Lord, Lord" will enter the kingdom of heaven. It's good to call Jesus "Lord," but that is not enough. Religious clichés can be throwaway language that means nothing.

Jesus' message here is so important. I am scared for those who think they are Christians, but are not. I fear for those who will face God on judgment day and he will say to them, "I never knew you." I do not want that to happen to you. Jesus is quite plain.

Matthew 7:21

Not everyone who says to me, "Lord, Lord" will enter the kingdom of heaven, but only the one who does the will of my Father who is in heaven.

Is salvation by works? Of course not. The contrast is not between human good deeds and God's amazing grace, but between professing your opinions and giving your allegiance. Are you really following Jesus or just talking about it? It's not enough to admire Jesus or even factually agree that he is the Savior of the world. Have you bowed your knee to him as your personal Lord? We are saved by faith, but only faith that is followed by action is true faith. Saving faith is demonstrated by a transformed life in the Spirit's power.

On that final judgment day, Jesus says many people will protest saying:

Matthew 7:22

Lord, Lord, did we not prophesy in your name and in your name drive out demons and in your name perform many miracles?

They claimed to know Jesus, but he did not know them. Just going to church, even serving and giving money, do not make you a Christian. Jesus' response is chilling:

Matthew 7:23

Then I will tell them plainly, "I never knew you. Away from me, you evildoers!"

Can you imagine hearing Jesus say that to you? To a person you know? It is going to happen to some people. These people will be tragically surprised when they find themselves rejected from the kingdom of heaven. They really thought they had made it in. This is a disturbing truth from Jesus. It can cause sensitive people to question their salvation. "Am I really saved? When I die, will I go to heaven or not?"

This is the crucial question. I believe Jesus would rather you worry over it than for even one person to miss eternity with him. Could you be among those Jesus is talking about? You are a quasi-Christian. You might call yourself a Christian. You might think you are going to heaven. But you have never given your allegiance to Jesus Christ and your life shows it. On judgment day, will Jesus know you? I do not want you to hear: "I never knew you." If you have any doubt, make sure. Choose to follow Jesus. Take the narrow road.

At the end of the Sermon on the Mount, Jesus offers stability in the storms. He moves to his third paired illustration: from two roads and two trees to two houses. It is plausible that Jesus had personal experience in house construction. The point of the two houses is to obey Jesus' words because the house on the rock foundation stands in the storm, but the house on the sand foundation crashes.

Two Houses

Storms reveal truth. If our lives are built on sand, when the storms come, we will collapse. If our lives are built on solid rock, when the storms come, we will stand. One day, each one of us will face the storms of God's judgment. Will you stand or fall? Jesus says:

Matthew 7:24–29

Therefore everyone who hears these words of mine and puts them into practice is like a wise man who built his house on the rock. The rain came down, the streams rose, and the winds blew and beat against that house; yet it did not fall, because it had its foundation on the rock. But everyone who hears these words of mine and does not put them into practice is like a foolish man who built his house on sand. The rain came down, the streams rose, and the winds blew and beat against that house, and it fell with a great crash.

In the contrast between the two builders, let's look at what's the same and what's different. Both people hear Jesus' Word. Both come to church. Both experience the storm. One stands and one crashes. One is wise and one is foolish. What sets the two people apart? One crucial difference.

The locale of the sermon near the Sea of Galilee finds a natural setting for this illustration. The alluvial sand ringing the seashore was hard during the hot summer months. But in the rainy season torrential rains produced sudden flash floods in riverbeds. Wise, hardworking builders would dig down sometimes ten feet below the surface sand to the bedrock. Today in Florida some people have built on a poor foundation that has led to massive sinkholes. One sinkhole took down an entire condo unit in minutes. It crashed because it was not built on a solid foundation.

As a little boy, I loved to build sandcastles. I still do. My mom and dad would take us to Port Aransas on the Texas coast of the Gulf of Mexico. Little boys do not know that sandcastles are not lasting. I built what I thought was a spectacular sandcastle, but when the tide came in, the castle went down. When you build on sand, the house will not stand. A house on the sand and a house on the rock may look similar on the outside. Both seem attractive and clean, freshly painted perhaps. Are you building a sandcastle life? On what foundation is your life built?

The crucial difference between the two people in Jesus' illustration is that one person puts Jesus' teaching into practice and the other does not. The difference between the two is not merely hearing the message, but doing it. I'm reminded of an old saying, "The road to hell is paved with good intentions." You can hear the truth. You can know the truth, but if you do not act on the truth, your foundation is sand. If you hear what Jesus is saying and do not obey it, you are a fool. If you hear him and do it, you are wise.

Two roads, two trees and two houses. Two destinies: eternal life and destruction. When the storm of God's final judgment blows, the house built on sand will fall with a great crash. Jesus ends his sermon on this tragic note: a great crash. Either you will stand forever with God in heaven or you will crash forever away from him in hell. Settle your eternal destiny. It is time to decide. Trust in Jesus Christ as the rock of your life. Neutrality is impossible. Jesus calls for decision. If you have built your life on anything but Jesus Christ alone, you will be washed away by God's judgment storm into eternal hell. Not to decide is to make a decision, and not the right one. Everyone is on the wide road to destruction unless you have made a conscious choice to enter the narrow road.

We are saved by faith, but we are judged by works. If you are unsure of your salvation, your eternal destiny, make sure. What saves you is not words you say, but a decision of your heart to follow Jesus. This is the action step of faith. If you trust in Christ from your heart, then God saves you. Your eternal life is secure because it is based on Jesus, the rock. You will spend eternity with God in heaven.

After Jesus' sermon, Matthew, the gospel writer, adds a final comment:

Matthew 7:28–29

When Jesus had finished saying these things, the crowds were amazed at his teaching, because he taught as one who had authority, and not as their teachers of the law.

If you know who Jesus is, then you want to follow his narrow road because you know where it leads and you know who is speaking. Jesus calls us to be all-in disciples, holding nothing back. In the sermon, Jesus paints an amazing vision of being a new kind of people, people who love our enemies, go the extra mile, and store up treasure in heaven. People who are never the same.

Jesus' authority and power amazed the crowds and they amaze us today. If he were not God incarnate, imagine the audacity of going up on a mountain and calling people to follow you, a Jewish carpenter, as the King of the world. In the end, Jesus asks us the most fundamental question: What road are you on? In computer language, it is either 1 or 0. It is a binary decision, either-or.[37] There is no middle ground. Are you going to follow Jesus on the narrow road and find life or are you going to play around on the wide road and find destruction?

The only acceptable response to the Sermon on the Mount is to embrace Jesus and accept his challenge to do what he says. He calls us to be all in, people who hold nothing back.

Not long ago 21 kidnapped Egyptian Christians were martyred when they chose to follow Jesus all the way to death. The last words they said, as recorded on the video sent around the world, were "Lord Jesus Christ." One of their brothers, Beshir Kamel, thanked ISIS for not editing out the men's declaration of belief in Christ because he said this had strengthened his own faith. He added that their families are "congratulating one another" and not in despair. "We are proud to have this number of people from our village who have become martyrs." The 21 followed Jesus all in, holding nothing back, even to paying the ultimate price.

If we answer Jesus' call, we will find divine blessings, a full life now and forever. Build your life on the solid rock. Choose the narrow road because Jesus, the King, is the one giving the challenge. And he is more than worth it. You will never be the same.

▌

For further study on chapter 8, see page 173.

Study Guide

This Study Guide will deepen your understanding of Jesus' Sermon on the Mount and thus increase your spiritual growth. To enrich your growth, I encourage you to do the study with others so you can encourage and sharpen each other. We grow best in community.

The WISDOM Process©

As children of God living in a hostile world, we need to learn how to think like Christ with biblical, spiritual wisdom for life.

Tested by thousands of people and hundreds of groups, the six-step WISDOM Process offers a surprisingly simple and profoundly powerful way to think. Today we are drowning in data and starving for wisdom. We Google for information on any topic, but we cannot find wisdom for life's complex challenges. This simple process can guide you to wisdom.

You will find that you can use The WISDOM Process not only in this Bible study but also for issues you face in ordinary life.

In order to accelerate your learning, this Study Guide employs The WISDOM Process. This process of thinking helps us move from knowing facts to transforming our lives in God's power. Most adults learn differently than children. Research into adult learning and studies of ancient education both show that people learn best when they have a reason to learn: a question to answer, a problem to solve or a mystery to unravel. All of us have these in our lives.

Role of Prayer

We access the guidance of God's Spirit through prayer and the Word of God. While God wants us to use our minds to study his Word to gain his revealed life direction, the Bible tells us:

James 1:5

If any of you lacks wisdom, he should ask God, who gives generously to all without finding fault, and it will be given to him.

Bible study should be covered with prayer. Paul prayed like this for the Colossians:

Colossians 1:9

For this reason, since the day we heard about you, we have not stopped praying for you and asking God to fill you with the knowledge of his will through all spiritual wisdom and understanding.

In answer to your prayers, the Spirit will shape your desires and then you will develop the mind of Christ. Rather than prayer being a specific step in The WISDOM Process, it should be threaded throughout the process of your study from start to end.

You will find that as you pray, the Spirit of God will guide you to truth. As a group, if you will prayerfully listen to the Spirit, he will direct your conversation to deep spiritual wisdom, conviction and motivation to honor God in daily life choices.

W Work the issue: *What's really at stake?*

Prepare your heart and mind before engaging God's Word. Take a moment to pray about questions in your life and issues arising from the Scripture you are studying. Consider how the Lord may want to impact you at this time. Bring your questions to your study of God's Word.

I Investigate Scripture: *What does God say?*

God's Word is our authority for life. It is our guide for belief and behavior. Our lives must be grounded in the Word of God. It is our primary source of absolute, divine truth. Spend time prayerfully and carefully considering what the biblical text is saying.

S Seek counsel: *What do wise people say?*

After studying the Scripture for ourselves, it is wise to seek the counsel of others. In Proverbs, Solomon said there is wisdom in a multitude of counselors. Wise people listen to advice (Proverbs 12:15; 13:10; 19:20). We provide you with well researched input in these chapters to help you understand God's Word better, but of course this counsel itself must be judged by the Word of God. We also provide a video message of each chapter.

D Develop your response: *What do I think?*

We learn best when we actively engage. Writing down answers to questions will deepen your interaction with God's Word. Some questions are designed to increase your understanding of the

Scripture; others help you extend your thinking in applying God's Word to your life.

O Openly discuss: *What do we think?*

Life transformation is increased when we sharpen each other in dynamic discussion. You will grow more if you study with a group where you can wrestle together with how to understand and obey God's Word. Together, prepared people led by the Holy Spirit will generate a dynamic in which ideas and wisdom multiply beyond what any individual could produce.

M Move to action: *What will I do?*

Christ calls us to obey all he commands (Matthew 28:20). The point of Bible study is not simply knowledge, but obedience. We are studying God's Word to be more and more conformed to the image of Jesus Christ to grow to maturity. The Bible tells us that hearing the Word without acting on it is like building a house on sand, while acting on the truth is like building a house on rock (Matthew 7:24–27; James 1:22–25). We are in the business of building houses on the Rock! Our study should lead us to move to action in the Spirit's power.

CHAPTER ONE

You Are the Light of the World Study Guide

Matthew 5:1–16

Pray

Prepare your heart and mind before engaging God's Word. Take a moment to pray about questions in your life and issues arising from the Scripture you are studying.

W Work the issue: *What's really at stake*?

Most people want to live a happy life, many want a life that matters, that makes a difference. Jesus addresses that kind of life in the Sermon on the Mount, only his ideas are far different from the majority voices in our world today.

What does a well lived life really look like? When the calendar turns over on January 1, it is common to set New Year's Resolutions.

Whatever you think of that tradition, how do most people's resolutions compare with the kinds of resolutions that would come from Jesus' address?

Jesus gives eight "Beatitudes," or blessings, to people who live a certain way and to each he offers a divine reward. Taken together, what kind of life do these eight traits depict? How would our lives have to change if we really lived out these eight Beatitudes? How might people around us respond?

What's at stake? What is the central issue or issues being addressed? What is the biggest issue for you?

Write down the main issue(s):

I Investigate Scripture: *What does God say?*

Read the verses slowly underlining what seems important to you. You will benefit from reading it several times. Mark key words. I encourage you to engage God in his Word. A good way to do that is to compare several English translations of the Bible. To easily compare various English translations, I recommend YouVersion as a good Bible reading app. In your study, it will help you to compare the New International Version, English Standard Version, Holman Christian Standard Bible and the New Living Translation, especially for a line or verse that is hard to understand.

Matthew 5:1–16

Now when Jesus saw the crowds, he went up on a mountainside and sat down. His disciples came to him, [2]and he began to teach them.

He said:

[3]"Blessed are the poor in spirit,
for theirs is the kingdom of heaven.
[4]Blessed are those who mourn,
for they will be comforted.
[5]Blessed are the meek,
for they will inherit the earth.
[6]Blessed are those who hunger and thirst for righteousness,
for they will be filled.
[7]Blessed are the merciful,
for they will be shown mercy.
[8]Blessed are the pure in heart,
for they will see God.
[9]Blessed are the peacemakers,
for they will be called children of God.
[10]Blessed are those who are persecuted because of righteousness,
for theirs is the kingdom of heaven.

[11]Blessed are you when people insult you, persecute you and falsely say all kinds of evil against you because of me. [12] Rejoice and be glad, because great is your reward in heaven, for in the same way they persecuted the prophets who were before you.

[13]You are the salt of the earth. But if the salt loses its saltiness, how can it be made salty again? It is no longer

good for anything, except to be thrown out and trampled underfoot.

[14]You are the light of the world. A town built on a hill cannot be hidden. [15] Neither do people light a lamp and put it under a bowl. Instead they put it on its stand, and it gives light to everyone in the house. [16] In the same way, let your light shine before others, that they may see your good deeds and glorify your Father in heaven.

- What traits, characteristics or attitudes will be rewarded by God?

- What rewards will be given to those who are "blessed"?

- List the types of people and their specific rewards.

- How are verses 3 and 10 related?

- What parallel phrasing do you see in verses 13 and 14?

- What metaphors does Jesus use in this Bible passage?

S Seek counsel: *What do wise people say?*

Read chapter 1 beginning on page 1 or watch a video presentation of this chapter. Access the QR (Quick Response) code that can be read by many smart devices using a scanning app. It allows you to immediately watch the video. If you do not have a QR code reader, you can access the same material at www.brucebmiller.com/neverthesame/chapter1_lightoftheworld. To the extent you have time and ability, read the relevant section from one of the recommended commentaries. Also check out the resources available on Bible.org.

D Develop your response: *What do I think?*

- What does Jesus mean by the term, "blessed"?

- Pick one Beatitude and elaborate on what it would be like today for a person to truly live out that trait.

- How can you be a brighter light for Jesus?

O Openly discuss: *What do we think?*

When you meet with your friend or group, walk through the following questions together but do not be limited by them. Prayerfully allow the Spirit of God to guide your conversation as you seek God together in his Word.

1. As we enter into this new study, what are your thoughts, feelings and questions about the Sermon on the Mount? What are your hopes for this study?

2. What does it mean to be "blessed" by God? Why is that valuable or important to you?

3. Read through the eight Beatitudes and pick a few to discuss at greater length using the following questions:

    a. How has this Beatitude been misunderstood or how could it be misconstrued?
    b. What does it mean as Jesus intends it?
    c. What is the blessing promised and why is that blessing of value?
    d. How could you better establish this quality in your life, such as being poor in spirit or pure in heart?

4. How can a person rejoice and be glad when they are insulted and persecuted for Christ?

5. How are the metaphors of salt and light related? What is Jesus' point?

6. How can we better shine our lights? To whom?

M Move to action: *What will I do?*

In reflecting on your study of Matthew 5:1–6, how will you move to action? God calls us not just to know his Word, but also to obey it, to be transformed by it through his Spirit. How do you believe God wants to change you through this text? Write down what you will do differently. This could be a transformation in your mind, in your heart, in your actions or in a relationship with another person.

Specifically,

- Which one of the Beatitudes in verses 3–11 will you work on developing this week in the Spirit's power? What are a few actions that will demonstrate that you are growing in that trait?

- How will you be saltier salt and brighter light to the people with whom you come in contact this week?

CHAPTER TWO

Go and Be Reconciled Study Guide

Matthew 5:27–37

W Work the issue: *What's really at stake?*

Scan the passage considering what underlying issues may be present. Reflect on what the author might be addressing in his time, and about you today. What questions does this text raise?

Where do we see anger in our world today? In our personal lives and homes? Since the Bible speaks about God getting angry, all anger must not be wrong. And yet anger often seems sinful and leads to sinful actions. Jesus addresses anger in the context of murder. How do we approach anger in a godly way?

Before he gets to anger, Jesus lays groundwork by talking about his relationship to the Old Testament law. Some Christians disagree and many are confused about how we are to relate to the Old Testament law today, especially the dietary law. Can we eat pork? Is the law still valid today or is it superseded by the coming of Jesus Christ?

Jesus' final point in this passage calls people to a high standard for reconciliation with your adversary, and even with anyone who has something against you.

What's at stake? What is the central issue or issues being addressed? What is the biggest issue for you?

Write down the main issue(s):

I Investigate Scripture: *What does God say?*

Read the passage slowly underlining what seems important to you. You will benefit from reading it several times. Mark key transition words such as "but," "for" and "therefore." Note carefully how Jesus describes his relationship to the Old Testament.

Matthew 5:17–26

Do not think that I have come to abolish the Law or the Prophets; I have not come to abolish them but to fulfill them. [18]For truly I tell you, until heaven and earth disappear, not the smallest letter, not the least stroke of a pen, will by any means disappear from the Law until everything is accomplished. [19]Therefore anyone who sets aside one of the least of these commands and teaches others accordingly will be called least in the kingdom of heaven, but whoever practices and teaches these commands will be called great in the kingdom of heaven. [20]For I tell you that unless your righteousness surpasses that of the Pharisees and the teachers of the law, you will certainly not enter the kingdom of heaven.

[21]You have heard that it was said to the people long ago, "You shall not murder, and anyone who murders will be subject to judgment." But I tell you that anyone who is angry with a brother or sister will be subject to judgment. Again, anyone who says to a brother or sister, "Raca," is answerable to the court. And anyone who says, "You fool!" will be in danger of the fire of hell.

[23]Therefore, if you are offering your gift at the altar and there remember that your brother or sister has something against you, [24]leave your gift there in front of the altar. First go and be reconciled to them; then come and offer your gift.

[25]Settle matters quickly with your adversary who is taking you to court. Do it while you are still together on the way, or your adversary may hand you over to the officer, and you may be thrown into prison. [26]Truly I tell you, you will not get out until you have paid the last penny.

- How does Jesus relieve fears that he might overturn the Mosaic Law (verses 17–18)?

- What is the standard for entering Jesus' kingdom?

- How does Jesus relate anger to murder?

- What are we to do if we are worshipping and remember that someone has something against us?

- How are we to settle matters with an adversary?

- What are consequences in this passage for violating what Jesus says?

S Seek counsel: *What do wise people say?*

Read chapter 2 beginning on page 19 or watch a video presentation of this chapter. Access the QR (Quick Response) code that can be read by many smart devices using a scanning app. It allows you to immediately watch the video. If you do not have a QR code reader, you can access the same material at www.brucebmiller.com/neverthesame/chapter2_goreconcile.
To the extent you have time and ability, read the relevant section from one of the recommended commentaries. Also check out the resources available on Bible.org.

D Develop your response: *What do I think?*

- Describe Jesus' relationship to the Old Testament Law in a few brief sentences or bullet points.

- Where is anger the biggest issue in your life? List with whom, when and where you most often get angry?

- Who are you aware of that has something against you? What could you do to reconcile with that person?

O Openly discuss: *What do we think?*

1. How do people tend to wrongly view the Old Testament today?

2. According to Matthew 5, what is the relationship of Jesus to "the Law and the prophets" (the Old Testament)? Explain.

3. What level of righteousness must we exhibit to enter the kingdom of heaven? With the teaching of the rest of the New Testament in view, how can anyone be that righteous?

4. What must one do to be called great in the kingdom of heaven?

5. How does Jesus take the command against murder to a deeper level?

6. In what situations, or with what people do you most often get angry? Who do you say angry words to the most? How will you change?

7. How would you retell Jesus' final two brief stories in your own words (verses 23–26)? With whom do you need to reconcile? What will you do and when will you do it?

M Move to action: *What will I do?*

- Based on what you learned in the discussion, refine your brief statement about Jesus' relationship to the Old Testament Law so it is clear in your own mind.

- Pray to the Father about giving your anger to him, and about having the strength to reconcile with anyone who has something against you or is your "adversary."

- Go reconcile with a person with whom you are in conflict, or who has something against you.

CHAPTER THREE

Let Your Yes Be Yes

Matthew 5:27–37

Pray

W Work the issue: *What's really at stake?*

There are many huge issues facing us today, but three tear apart our families: lust, divorce and lying. Each of them Jesus addresses with a call to drastic action. How are all three related? As you look out into the culture around you, and into your own family, what negative consequences do you see resulting from lust, divorce and lying? Begin to imagine a community transformed by Jesus where everyone is characterized by purity, commitment and truthfulness. What would that look like in your life, your family, your church? In your own life, which of these has created the most pain? In which of these three areas are you most motivated to do something, even if it is drastic, to obey Jesus?

What's at stake? What is the central issue or issues being addressed? What is the biggest issue for you?

Write down the main issue(s):

Investigate Scripture: *What does God say?*

Matthew 5:27–37

You have heard that it was said, "You shall not commit adultery." [28]*But I tell you that anyone who looks at a woman lustfully has already committed adultery with her in his heart.* [2] *If your right eye causes you to stumble, gouge it out and throw it away. It is better for you to lose one part of your body than for your whole body to be thrown into hell.* [3] *And if your right hand causes you to stumble, cut it off and throw it away. It is better for you to lose one part of your body than for your whole body to go into hell.*

[31]*It has been said, "Anyone who divorces his wife must give her a certificate of divorce."* [32]*But I tell you*

that anyone who divorces his wife, except for sexual immorality, makes her the victim of adultery, and anyone who marries a divorced woman commits adultery.

[33]Again, you have heard that it was said to the people long ago, "Do not break your oath, but fulfill to the Lord the vows you have made." [34]But I tell you, do not swear an oath at all: either by heaven, for it is God's throne; [35]or by the earth, for it is his footstool; or by Jerusalem, for it is the city of the Great King. [36]And do not swear by your head, for you cannot make even one hair white or black. [37]All you need to say is simply "Yes" or "No"; anything beyond this comes from the evil one.

- Do you think Jesus is being literal or figurative when he speaks of tearing out your eye and cutting off your hand? What is the point he is making?

- Describe how Jesus uses a self-interest argument in verses 29–30.

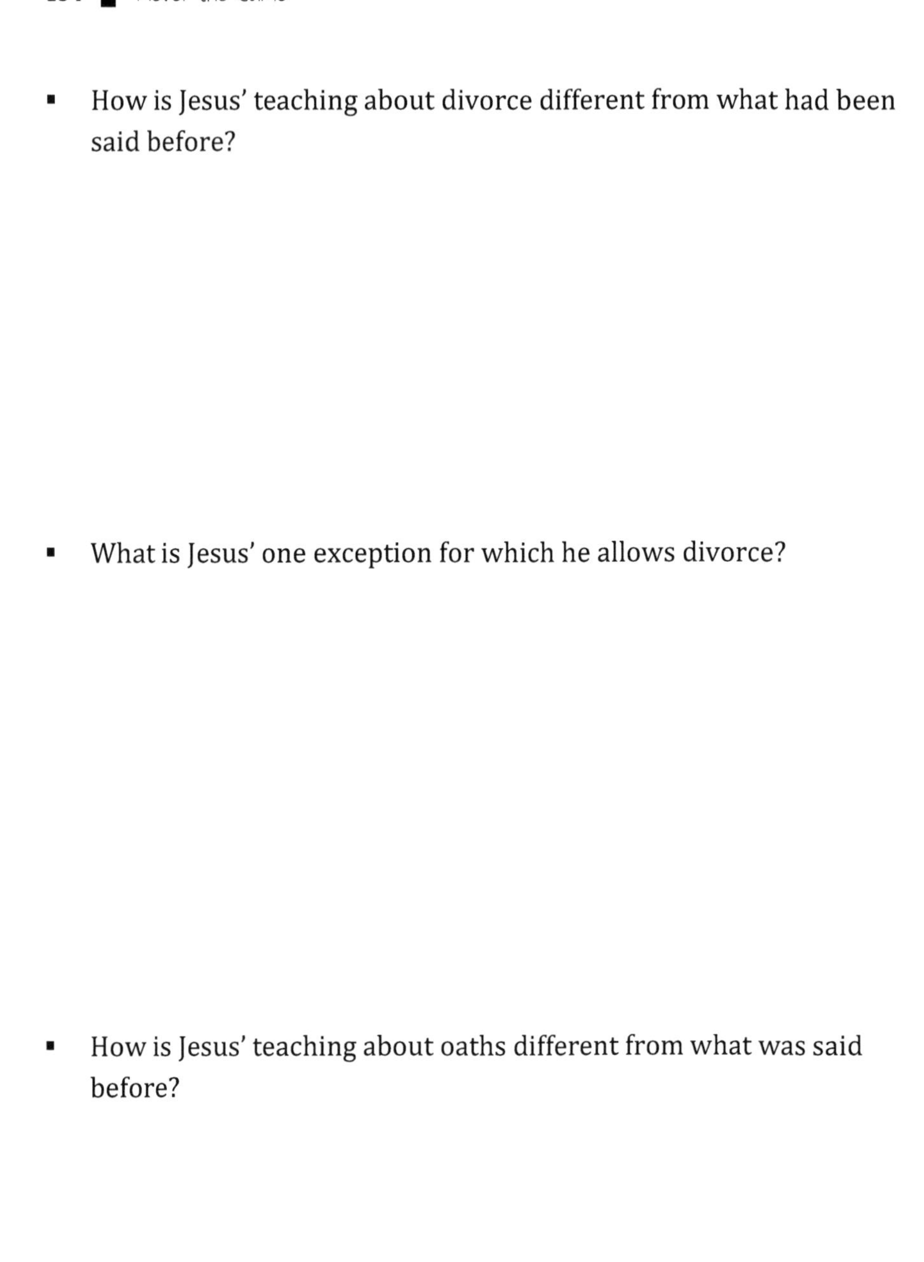

- How is Jesus' teaching about divorce different from what had been said before?

- What is Jesus' one exception for which he allows divorce?

- How is Jesus' teaching about oaths different from what was said before?

- After Jesus says what not to do in regard to oaths, what is the one thing we need to do?

S Seek counsel: *What do wise people say?*

Read chapter 3 on page 31 or watch a video presentation of this chapter. Access the QR (Quick Response) code that can be read by many smart devices using a scanning app. It allows you to immediately watch the video. If you do not have a QR code reader, you can access the same material at www.brucebmiller.com/neverthesame/chapter3_yesbeyes. To the extent you have time and ability, read the relevant section from one of the recommended commentaries. Also check out the resources available on Bible.org.

D Develop your response: *What do I think?*

- What drastic action could you take to rip lust out of your life?

- If you are not married, write out a brief statement of your conviction about the permanence of marriage. If you are married, write down one action you could take to protect your marriage from divorce.

- Identify where in your life you most commonly fudge the truth. In what arenas or situations are you tempted to tell less than the whole truth? Then determine by God's Spirit to simply tell the truth in those cases.

O Openly discuss: *What do we think*?

1. Of these three, which do you think is the most damaging in your community: lust, divorce or lying?

2. What does Jesus say constitutes adultery in our hearts? How would you distinguish mental adultery (lust) from temptation?

3. Jesus gives two graphic illustrations, drastic actions with our eyes and hands, to get rid of lustful desiring. What examples can you give of drastic measures we could take today to avoid lust? What do you need to cut out of your life?

4. What is Jesus saying about marriage and divorce? What are valid and invalid reasons to get divorced?

5. In Matthew 5:33–37, Jesus' point is that we should stay true to our word. Where in our lives are lies most common? What casual promises do we make without real intentions of following through? What kinds of word games or rationalizations do we use to justify not keeping our word? Where do you need to grow in staying true to your word?

6. From all that Jesus says about staying pure in your heart, committed to your spouse and true to your word, where are you most convicted? Are there sins you feel comfortable confessing right now?

7. After we receive God's amazing gracious forgiveness in Jesus Christ for our sin, we then freshly consecrate (dedicate) ourselves to follow Jesus, holding nothing back. In view of this passage, where will you consecrate yourself to more fully follow Jesus Christ?

M Move to action: *What will I do?*

- What action, even drastic, will you take to remove lust from your heart?

- Where will you pledge to tell the truth no matter what?

Turn the Other Cheek Study Guide

Matthew 5:38–48

W Work the issue: *What's really at stake?*

One unique characteristic of American society is that we insist on "standing up for our rights." In modern times, there are numerous groups formed to protect rights. We have organizations dedicated to protect and promote civil rights, women's rights, employee rights, tenant rights and a host of others. We are a generation obsessed with upholding our rights.

We idolize action heroes who fight for their rights regardless of the cost. Actors such as Charles Bronson, Sylvester Stallone, Jean-

Claude Van Damme, Arnold Schwarzenegger, Bruce Willis, and Liam Neeson have made a host of movies with plot lines of revenge and retaliation. Unfortunately, that "Don't mess with me" spirit reflects our sin.

Jesus raises the standard in ending disputes and loving our enemies. This change goes against our natural impulses. It goes against our tendency to insist on our rights and hate our enemies. Instead, we are to be channels of humility and love. People who turn the other cheek and go the extra mile.

What's at stake? What is the central issue or issues being addressed? What is the biggest issue for you?

Write down the main issue(s):

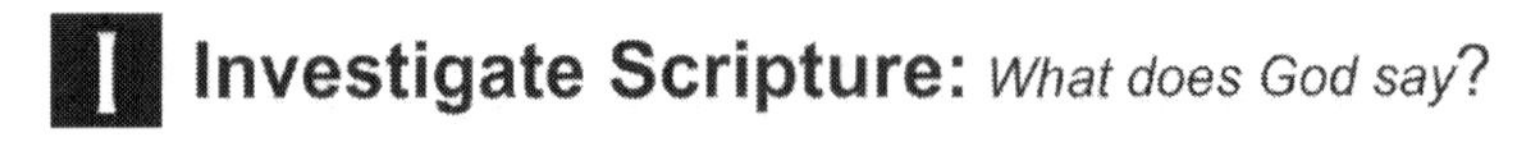

I Investigate Scripture: *What does God say?*

Matthew 5:38–48

You have heard that it was said, "Eye for eye, and tooth for tooth." [39]But I tell you, do not resist an evil person. If anyone slaps you on the right cheek, turn to them the other cheek also. [40]And if anyone wants to sue you and take your shirt, hand over your coat as well. [41]If anyone forces you to go one mile, go with them two miles. [42]Give to the one who asks you, and do not turn away from the one who wants to borrow from you.

[43]You have heard that it was said, "Love your neighbor and hate your enemy." [44]But I tell you, love your enemies and pray for those who persecute you, [45]that you may be children of your Father in heaven. He causes his sun to rise on the evil and the good, and sends rain on the righteous and the unrighteous. [46]If you love those who love you, what reward will you get? Are not even the tax collectors doing that? [47]And if you greet only your own people, what are you doing more than others? Do not even pagans do that? [48]Be perfect, therefore, as your heavenly Father is perfect.

- How does Jesus go beyond "eye for an eye" teaching?

- What do verses 40–43 have in common?

- How does Jesus go beyond "love your neighbor and hate your enemy"?

- What is our motivation, or goal, for loving our enemies according to verse 45?

- In what concrete ways are we to love our enemies or those different from us?

- By using questions, what reason(s) does Jesus give in verses 46–47?

- What is Jesus' final command in Matthew 5?

S Seek counsel: *What do wise people say?*

Read chapter 4 beginning on page 43 or watch a video presentation of this chapter. Access the QR (Quick Response) code that can be read by many smart devices using a scanning app. It allows you to immediately watch the video. If you do not have a QR code reader, you can access the same material at www.brucebmiller.com/neverthesame/chapter4_turncheek.
To the extent you have time and ability, read the relevant section from one of the recommended commentaries. Also check out the resources available on Bible.org.

D Develop your response: *What do I think?*

- In reviewing Jesus' five illustrations in verses 38–42, which one do you most need to put into practice? What will that look like in your life today?

- Think of an "enemy" in your life or someone who has hurt you and pray blessings for them. Pray for the sun to shine on their life and the rain to come bringing prosperity.

- As you consider the people you encounter in your weekly life, are there any you avoid? Write down someone you could warmly greet who is different from you.

Openly discuss: *What do we think?*

1. Where is revenge most common in our culture? In our personal lives? When someone hurts you, what do you want to do? Why?

2. How does Jesus counter the old teaching of "an eye for an eye"? How is his way of life different?

3. Jesus uses five examples of not resisting an evil person. Pick a few of the five to spend more time on. For each one ask: What does it mean? What principle is Jesus illustrating with his historical example? What are examples today of how to apply this in our lives? And what do you need to do differently, with whom?

    - Insults—Turn the other cheek
    - Injustice—Give your coat
    - Imposition—Go the second mile
    - Request for money—Give it
    - Desire to borrow something—Lend it

4. Jesus says we are to love our enemies. Who might be considered a person's "enemy" in today's world? In our daily lives?

5. Jesus says to pray for those who hurt you. Have you ever done that? What makes it hard? What might be the benefits? For whom could you commit to pray blessings?

6. Jesus says to greet people different from us. Who do you tend to avoid? Who could you warmly greet who is different from you?

7. As his children, we are to be like our heavenly Father. How does Jesus describe our heavenly Father? How can we be like that too?

M Move to action: *What will I do?*

- What action in your life would be the equivalent of turning your cheek, giving the coat off your back, or going the extra mile? And to whom will you demonstrate this godly behavior?

- What enemy will you pray for this week?

- Who will you warmly greet who is different from you?

There is not an abundance of people willing to live this way. You will stand out for God and his message.

CHAPTER FIVE

Your Kingdom Come Study Guide

Matthew 6:1–8

Pray

W Work the issue: *What's really at stake?*

Some people's religious activities are nothing more than a show designed to convince others of their supposed spirituality. But God rejects such actions as a sham, knowing that the object of their devotion is really themselves and not him. Some of the scribes and Pharisees were experts at this hypocrisy.

A question posed by this week's study is this: "Who will give you a reward?" In the passage, three religious actions are described—giving, praying and fasting. You can perform them as an act of devotion to God and receive his reward, or you can do them to be noticed by people and receive their acclaim.

Some people worry about praying in public. Many are anxious that no one know about their giving. Is it appropriate to pray in public, or to let anyone know how much you give? How can we "let our light shine" and yet not do religious deeds in front of people so they see us?

What's at stake? What is the central issue or issues being addressed? What is the biggest issue for you?

Write down the main issue(s):

I Investigate Scripture: *What does God say?*

Matthew 6:1–18

Be careful not to practice your righteousness in front of others to be seen by them. If you do, you will have no reward from your Father in heaven.

[2]So when you give to the needy, do not announce it with trumpets, as the hypocrites do in the synagogues

and on the streets, to be honored by others. Truly I tell you, they have received their reward in full. [3]But when you give to the needy, do not let your left hand know what your right hand is doing, [4]so that your giving may be in secret. Then your Father, who sees what is done in secret, will reward you.

[5]And when you pray, do not be like the hypocrites, for they love to pray standing in the synagogues and on the street corners to be seen by others. Truly I tell you, they have received their reward in full. [6]But when you pray, go into your room, close the door and pray to your Father, who is unseen. Then your Father, who sees what is done in secret, will reward you. [7]And when you pray, do not keep on babbling like pagans, for they think they will be heard because of their many words. [8]Do not be like them, for your Father knows what you need before you ask him.

[9]This, then, is how you should pray:

"Our Father in heaven,
hallowed be your name,
[10]your kingdom come,
your will be done,
on earth as it is in heaven.
[11]Give us today our daily bread.
[12]And forgive us our debts,
as we also have forgiven our debtors.
[13]And lead us not into temptation,
but deliver us from the evil one."

[14]For if you forgive other people when they sin against you, your heavenly Father will also forgive you. [15]But if you do not forgive others their sins, your Father will not forgive your sins.

[16]When you fast, do not look somber as the hypocrites do, for they disfigure their faces to show

others they are fasting. Truly I tell you, they have received their reward in full. [17]But when you fast, put oil on your head and wash your face, [18]so that it will not be obvious to others that you are fasting, but only to your Father, who is unseen; and your Father, who sees what is done in secret, will reward you.

- The text above is divided into three general subjects. What are they?

- What motive lurks behind the action in verses 1, 5 and 16?

- What common theme do we find that results from being noticed by others?

- Which phrases point to a public setting?

- Which phrases point to a private setting?

- What is common to how Jesus says we are we to give, pray and fast? And what is the result for us?

- How does the Lord's Prayer divide into two sets of three petitions each? List each petition in your own words.

S Seek counsel: *What do wise people say?*

Read chapter 5 beginning on page 55 or watch a video presentation of this chapter. Access the QR (Quick Response) code that can be read by many smart devices using a scanning app. It allows you to immediately watch the video. If you do not have a QR code reader, you can access the same material at www.brucebmiller.com/neverthesame/chapter5_yourkingdom. To the extent you have time and ability, read the relevant section from one of the recommended commentaries. Also check out the resources available on Bible.org.

D Develop your response: *What do I think?*

- Prayerfully examine your own heart for why you engage in spiritual activities. To what extent are your motives to honor God, and to what extent are they to make yourself look good to others?

- Research your records and write down how much money you have given to your local church this year. What percent of your income does that represent? What, if any, change will you make to your giving so that you are giving more generously and proportionately as God has blessed you?

- Take time to pray in accord with the model of the Lord's Prayer.

Bonus: Experiment with a spiritual fast.

O Openly discuss: *What do we think?*

1. Where do you see religion demonstrated publicly among American Christians in which a person is trying to act spiritual for others to see? In your own life? Let's be honest with each other.

2. Jesus addresses three topics in this order: giving, praying and fasting. While he addresses motives, he assumes we are giving, praying and fasting. Let's start with the basics.

    a. Do you give to your church? How often? Roughly, what percent of your income do you give to your church? To all charitable causes?
    b. Do you pray? How often? For how long?
    c. Have you ever fasted?

3. Jesus drives to the motives behind giving, praying and fasting. At issue is audience: other people or God. Giving and praying are commanded in the New Testament. How would you evaluate your heart attitude in your giving? Your praying? Or your fasting?

4. There is a tension between Jesus' teachings to let our light shine (5:16) and not to do our righteousness in front of others. How can we reconcile this apparent conflict?

5. Describe the model for prayer that Jesus gives in the Lord's Prayer. How do your prayers compare with his model?

6. If you have fasted, share the experience with the group and how it benefited you spiritually.

7. If you are not where you know the Lord wants you to be in your giving or praying, what's one step you could take to grow in giving or praying so you are more faithful to Christ?

M Move to action: *What will I do?*

- Spend some time with the Lord inviting him to shine a light on your heart to examine the motives behind your spiritual actions.

- Ask the Lord to cleanse your heart of self-centered motives and transform your heart to desire his honor above others' opinions of you.

- Take concrete action to improve your giving or praying. What one next step will you take? Then share it with one other person so they can pray for you and encourage you.

CHAPTER SIX

You Cannot Serve Two Masters Study Guide

Matthew 6:19–34

Pray

W Work the issue: *What's really at stake?*

Money and worry dog most all of us, and are often related to each other. In this passage, Jesus addresses attitudes toward materialism. The rich are tempted to trust in their possessions, and the poor are tempted to doubt God's provision. Both worry, if only for different reasons. How should a Christ follower view money? Jesus talks about earthly and heavenly treasures, so how does an eternal perspective make a difference? In our society, what role does money and what it can buy, play in how we conduct our lives? How should Christians look at money differently? How is money an issue in your life, your marriage or family?

What about worry? In what ways are money and worry often connected? What do you most worry about? Jesus gives us seven reasons not to worry. What could possibly knock worry out of our minds? Rather than worrying about money, on the positive side, what are we to do instead?

What's at stake? What is the central issue or issues being addressed? What is the biggest issue for you?

> Write down the main issue(s):

I Investigate Scripture: *What does God say?*

Matthew 6:19–30

Do not store up for yourselves treasures on earth, where moths and vermin destroy, and where thieves break in and steal. [20]But store up for yourselves treasures in heaven, where moths and vermin do not destroy, and where thieves do not break in and steal. [21]For where your treasure is, there your heart will be also.

[22]The eye is the lamp of the body. If your eyes are healthy, your whole body will be full of light. [23]But if your eyes are unhealthy, your whole body will be full of darkness. If then the light within you is darkness, how great is that darkness!

[24]No one can serve two masters. Either you will hate the one and love the other, or you will be devoted to the one and despise the other. You cannot serve both God and money.

[25]Therefore I tell you, do not worry about your life, what you will eat or drink; or about your body, what you will wear. Is not life more than food, and the body more than clothes? [26]Look at the birds of the air; they do not sow or reap or store away in barns, and yet your heavenly Father feeds them. Are you not much more valuable than they? [27]Can any one of you by worrying add a single hour to your life?

[28]And why do you worry about clothes? See how the flowers of the field grow. They do not labor or spin. [29]Yet I tell you that not even Solomon in all his splendor was dressed like one of these. [30]If that is how God clothes the grass of the field, which is here today and tomorrow is thrown into the fire, will he not much more clothe you—you of little faith?

- What metaphor is used in verse 19?

- What contrasts do you see in verses 19 and 20?

- What contrasts do you see in verses 22–23, and then verse 24?

- What rationales do you see in verses 19–24 for why we should obey what Jesus is saying? Look both for negative and positive consequences.

- How could you summarize Jesus' message in verses 25–32?

- List the metaphors and analogies that Jesus uses in verses 25–32?

- What is Jesus' final command in contrast with worry (33)? And why should we do it?

S Seek counsel: *What do wise people say?*

Read chapter 6 beginning on page 71 or watch a video presentation of this chapter. Access the QR (Quick Response) code that can be read by many smart devices using a scanning app. It allows you to immediately watch the video. If you do not have a QR code reader, you can access the same material at www.brucebmiller.com/neverthesame/chapter6_twomasters. To the extent you have time and ability, read the relevant section from one of the recommended commentaries. Also check out the resources available on Bible.org.

D Develop your response: *What do I think?*

- Take sufficient time to prayerfully invite God to examine your heart about money and what money can buy. Ask him to help you see to what extent you are "serving" money, storing up treasures on earth. Then confess what you need to confess. And pledge to serve God alone, storing up treasure in heaven that will last. If it helps you, write out your prayer to God.

- List the things you most worry about. Take these to the Lord in prayer. Then write down in your own words the most compelling arguments to you in Jesus' teaching regarding why we should not worry.

Openly discuss: *What do we think?*

1. What evidences do you see around you that people in our society "serve" money? How do we "store up treasure" on "earth"? How do you do this?

2. What are ways we can invest in heavenly treasure? And why is that better than storing up earthly treasure?

3. How is what we do with our treasures tied to our heart? Why can we not serve God and money? How do we try to do that?

4. How is Matthew 6:19–24 related to the next paragraph in verses 25–32?

5. In what areas of your life are you prone to worry? What do you worry about the most often?

6. In verses 25–32, Jesus gives seven reasons not to worry. Which ones are most compelling to you? Why?

7. What is Jesus' conclusion to the chapter? What next step can you take with your money (treasures) to more fully seek first God's righteous rule?

M Move to action: *What will I do?*

- Take time again to prayerfully bring your heart about money before the Lord in prayer.

- Take a concrete action to store up your treasures in heaven rather than on earth.

- Pick one reason not to worry and a verse to memorize and meditate on.

CHAPTER SEVEN

Do Not Judge Study Guide

Matthew 7:1–12

Pray

W Work the issue: *What's really at stake?*

Jesus gives two of his most famous ethical principles in this passage, principles people love to quote at other people, more than apply to themselves. They are "Do not judge" and "Do unto others as you would have them do unto you," the so-called Golden Rule. In modern culture, these are two of the most misused, abused and ignored quotes from the Sermon on the Mount.

It's ironic that Christians have been judged by contemporary critics as being horribly judgmental. And yet while we can dismiss over-the-top and off-the-mark judgments against us, we would do better to face the grains of truth there. All too often Christians have been judgmental of others. Some grossly so in public places, recorded by the media for all to see and groan over. And yet are we not to make judgments about what is morally good and not? About what is true and what is heresy? How can we judge without being judgmental? How do you find yourself most prone to judge? How have you been judged by others?

In concluding this passage, Jesus calls us to pray to our Father and he summarizes his message. What is his point about prayer, and how often do we get it wrong? How is the Golden Rule a summary of the sermon?

What's at stake? What is the central issue or issues being addressed? What is the biggest issue for you?

Write down the main issue(s):

Investigate Scripture: *What does God say?*

Matthew 7:1–12

Do not judge, or you too will be judged. [2]For in the same way you judge others, you will be judged, and with the measure you use, it will be measured to you.

[3]Why do you look at the speck of sawdust in your brother's eye and pay no attention to the plank in your own eye? [4]How can you say to your brother, "Let me take

the speck out of your eye," when all the time there is a plank in your own eye? [5]You hypocrite, first take the plank out of your own eye, and then you will see clearly to remove the speck from your brother's eye.

[6]Do not give dogs what is sacred; do not throw your pearls to pigs. If you do, they may trample them under their feet, and turn and tear you to pieces.

[7]Ask and it will be given to you; seek and you will find; knock and the door will be opened to you. [8]For everyone who asks receives; the one who seeks finds; and to the one who knocks, the door will be opened.

[9]Which of you, if your son asks for bread, will give him a stone? [10]Or if he asks for a fish, will give him a snake? [11]If you, then, though you are evil, know how to give good gifts to your children, how much more will your Father in heaven give good gifts to those who ask him! [12]So in everything, do to others what you would have them do to you, for this sums up the Law and the Prophets.

- Explain verses 1–2 in your own words.

- How is Jesus' illustration related to his occupation, and also humorous? If you can draw (unlike me), sketch a picture of the exaggerated situation he is describing?

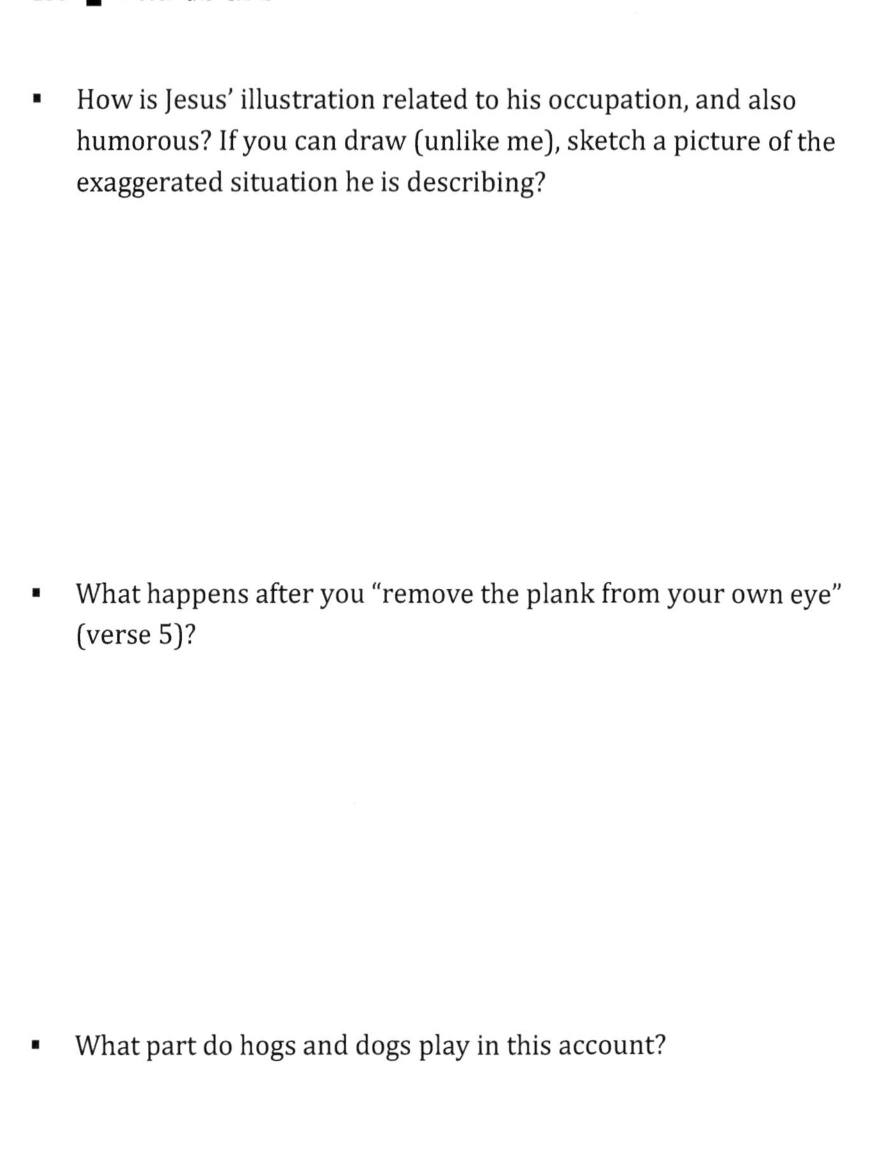

- What happens after you "remove the plank from your own eye" (verse 5)?

- What part do hogs and dogs play in this account?

- What is Jesus teaching us about prayer in verses 7–11?

- How does the Golden Rule sum up the law and the prophets (12)?

S Seek counsel: *What do wise people say?*

Read chapter 7 beginning on page 85 or watch a video presentation of this chapter. Access the QR (Quick Response) code that can be read by many smart devices using a scanning app. It allows you to immediately watch the video. If you do not have a QR code reader, you can access the same material at www.brucebmiller.com/neverthesame/chapter7_donotjudge. To the extent you have time and ability, read the relevant section from one of the recommended commentaries. Also check out the resources available on Bible.org.

D Develop your response: *What do I think?*

- Ask God to help you see how you judge others. Then write down the persons or kinds of people you are prone to judge. Confess your sin and receive God's gracious forgiveness in Christ.

- Write down in a few sentences how we *are* to judge and *are not* to judge.

- Ask God to show you a "plank" you need to remove from your eye. What name would you give that plank? Then ask the Lord to show you a friend with a speck that you could help them gently and lovingly remove.

O Openly discuss: *What do we think?*

1. Why do you think many unchurched people view Christians as judgmental?

2. In what ways have you been judged both fairly and unfairly? In what ways do we judge people?

3. Rather than condemning others, what does Jesus say we should do? What should we do first? What planks do you need to remove from your eye?

4. How can we appropriately remove another's "speck"?

5. What kind of people should we avoid helping to get out specks (verse 6)?

6. What do verses 7–11 teach us about God that encourages us to pray?

7. How does the Golden Rule (verse 12) summarize this section of the Sermon on the Mount? Compare Matthew 7:12 to 5:17. What is one way you could exercise the Golden Rule with one person this week?

M Move to action: *What will I do?*

- Determine before the Lord that you will stop judging a specific person or group of people.

- Take a specific "plank" out of your eye before you try to help a friend take a speck out of their eye.

CHAPTER EIGHT

Enter the Narrow Gate Study Guide

Matthew 7:13–29

 **Pray**

W Work the issue: *What's really at stake?*

An ancient expression tracing back to the 1300s says, "The proof of the pudding is in the eating." Literally, it means that you won't know whether the food has been cooked properly until you try it. Figuratively, it means not to assume that something is in order without verifying it. It's much the same idea as "seeing is believing" or "actions speak louder than words."

There are three elements in this saying: decisions regarding ingredients, a process of time and the final result. During the midst of the process, you may not be able to tell the outcome, but the final result will show if it was a success.

In our final passage, we see this principle repeated three times with two roads,, two trees and two builders. The passing of time reveals which is the right way, the good fruit, and the wise builder. The final results are eternal contrasting. As any good speaker would, Jesus finishes by asking for a commitment. Choose well and your life will be blessed now and forever, or not.

Where do you stand with Jesus? How would you characterize the level of your current commitment to him?

What's at stake? What is the central issue or issues being addressed? What is the biggest issue for you?

Write down the main issue(s):

I Investigate Scripture: *What does God say?*

Matthew 7:13–29

"Enter through the narrow gate. For wide is the gate and broad is the road that leads to destruction, and many enter through it. [14]But small is the gate and narrow the road that leads to life, and only a few find it.

[15]"Watch out for false prophets. They come to you in sheep's clothing, but inwardly they are ferocious wolves. [16]By their fruit you will recognize them. Do people pick grapes from thornbushes, or figs from thistles? [17]Likewise, every good tree bears good fruit, but a bad tree bears bad fruit. [18]A good tree cannot bear bad fruit, and a bad tree cannot bear good fruit. [19]Every tree that does not bear good fruit is cut down and thrown into the fire. [20] Thus, by their fruit you will recognize them.

[21]"Not everyone who says to me, 'Lord, Lord,' will enter the kingdom of heaven, but only the one who does the will of my Father who is in heaven. [22]Many will say to me on that day, 'Lord, Lord, did we not prophesy in your name and in your name drive out demons and in your name perform many miracles?' [23]Then I will tell them plainly, 'I never knew you. Away from me, you evildoers!'

[24]"Therefore everyone who hears these words of mine and puts them into practice is like a wise man who built his house on the rock. [25]The rain came down, the streams rose, and the winds blew and beat against that house; yet it did not fall, because it had its foundation on the rock. [26]But everyone who hears these words of mine and does not put them into practice is like a foolish man who built his house on sand. [27]The rain came down, the

streams rose, and the winds blew and beat against that house, and it fell with a great crash."

[28]When Jesus had finished saying these things, the crowds were amazed at his teaching, [29]because he taught as one who had authority, and not as their teachers of the law.

- What figures of speech or metaphorical language do you see in these verses?

- What outcomes are described in these verses?

- What contrasts do you find in verses 13–14? Put them in a simple chart.

- How are animals and plants used in verses 15–20?

- How would you state verse 21 in your own words?

- What claim will many people make before Jesus on judgment day according to verse 22? And yet what will he say to them?

- How would you compare and contrast what happened to each of the two houses?

- What were people's reactions to Jesus' sermon and why (28–29)?

S Seek counsel: *What do wise people say?*

Read chapter 8 beginning on page 97 or watch a video presentation of this chapter. Access the QR (Quick Response) code that can be read by many smart devices using a scanning app. It allows you to immediately watch the video. If you do not have a QR code reader, you can access the same material at www.brucebmiller.com/neverthesame/chapter8_narrowgate. To the extent you have time and ability, read the relevant section from one of the recommended commentaries. Also check out the resources available on Bible.org.

D Develop your response: *What do I think?*

- In your words, describe the choice that Jesus is putting before us in the conclusion of his Sermon on the Mount with his three illustrations?

- What is your choice in regard to the two roads, trees and houses? Write it down.

- What are implications of your choice for your daily life?

Openly discuss: *What do we think?*

1. What are your favorite sections or sayings in the Sermon on the Mount? Why?

2. How would you describe the two different roads that Jesus contrasts? Why do we find many on the wide road? What are the roads' different destinations? What (or who) is the narrow gate?

3. How can we recognize false prophets, teachers? What are examples of bad fruit? Of good fruit?

4. Who will be surprised that they do not enter the kingdom of heaven? What sorts of people might fit this category today? Are you sure you are saved? Why or why not?

5. BONUS: According to the New Testament, what is the relationship between faith and works ("doing the will of my Father who is in heaven")?

6. In Jesus' illustration of the two houses, what is the same and what is different? What one factor accounts for the different outcomes?

7. As he ends the sermon, Jesus uses three illustrations (two roads, two trees and two houses) to bring us to a point of decision. There are only two choices: follow him fully, or not. What is your decision?

M Move to action: *What will I do?*

- Choose to follow Jesus fully, all in, holding nothing back.

- Throughout the Sermon on the Mount, what is Jesus saying to you that you have heard but not acted upon?

Final Thoughts

The more I've studied Jesus' Sermon on the Mount, the more profoundly it challenges me. Every section presents a radical vision of what it looks like to follow Jesus. If we follow it, we will never be the same.

May the Lord press on your heart the transformation that the Spirit most wants in you at this time in your life. Then, through the rest of your life, I encourage you to return to Matthew 5–7 over and over again, because there is more truth than we will be able to plumb in a lifetime.

My hope and prayer is that more and more people will make the courageous decision to take Jesus seriously, and so follow him with no reservations or qualifications, all in, holding nothing back. May we never be the same!

This is real living. This honors God. And matters forever.

Bruce

Acknowledgments

In spite of his failings and some unwise teaching, God used Bill Gothard in his Basic Youth Conflicts Seminar, to challenge me to memorize Jesus' Sermon on the Mount. I remain grateful. It was the first large portion of Scripture I ever put to memory, and it has blessed me all my life.

I'm amazingly blessed to be the pastor of Christ Fellowship where I serve with a trusted team of Elders and Pastors, who are among my closest friends. Thank you for helping me to teach this series at our church, and enabling me to put it into this book. It's a joy to serve Jesus with you!

Once again it is a privilege to work with my editor, Iva Morelli, who encourages me, and challenges me to be better. Any mistakes are mine, not hers, but if you find them, let us know so we can fix them.

As I was writing these lines, my wonderful wife Tamara called. She is God's best earthly gift to me. Without her, this book would not exist. For over 30 years, she has been my partner, best friend and precious wife.

Most of all I am thankful to the triune God who created me, saved me and is one day coming to rule as the rightful King of this world.

Recommended Commentaries

Advanced

Grant R. Osborne, *Matthew, Zondervan Exegetical Commentary on the New Testament* (Grand Rapids: Zondervan, 2010).

David L. Turner, *Matthew, Baker Exegetical Commentary on the New Testament* (Grand Rapids: Baker Academic, 2008).

Craig L. Blomberg, *Matthew, The New American Commentary* (Nashville: Broadman Press, 1992).

Easier

William W. Klein, *Become What You Are: Spiritual Formation According to the Sermon on the Mount* (Tyrone, GA: Authentic Publishing, 2006).

Scot McKnight, *The Story of God Bible Commentary: Sermon on the Mount* (Grand Rapids: Zondervan, 2013).

About the Author

BRUCE B. MILLER

God has given Bruce the privilege of serving as husband to his wife, Tamara, since 1983 and father to their five children. They are also blessed with their grandchildren. God used Bruce to plant Christ Fellowship in McKinney, Texas where he currently serves as senior pastor (CFhome.org). In his spare time, he loves spending time with Tamara, playing racquetball, using a chainsaw and sitting by an open fire with his chocolate Labrador, Calvin.

His passion for leadership development led to his first book, *The Leadership Baton*, written with Jeff Jones and Rowland Forman. Bruce's heart to see people live more fulfilled lives sparked the writing of *Your Life in Rhythm*, the forerunner to *Your Church in Rhythm* which applies the concepts of rhythmic living to local churches (BruceBMiller.com).

Bruce developed the innovative six-step WISDOM Process© which serves as a learning engine in the study guides for his books *Big God in a Chaotic World—A Fresh Look at Daniel; When God Makes No Sense—A Fresh Look at Habakkuk;* and *Sexuality—Approaching Controversial Issues with Grace, Truth and Hope.*

Bruce graduated Phi Beta Kappa from the University of Texas at Austin with a B.A. in Plan II, the Honors Liberal Arts Program ('82); received a master's degree in Theology from Dallas Theological Seminary ('86); and did doctoral work at the University of Texas at Dallas in the History of Ideas (focus on philosophical hermeneutics, Hans-Georg Gadamer, and postmodernism). He taught theology for four years at Dallas Theological Seminary.

Bruce speaks and consults around the world. He founded the Centers for Church Based Training and served as Chairman of the Board for 12 years (http://ccbt.org). Bruce founded and leads Dadlin ministries, an organization committed to helping people develop wisdom for life.

You can follow Bruce:

Twitter (http://twitter.com/Bruce_B_Miller) or
Facebook (https://www.facebook.com/BruceBMillerAuthor)
Blog (BruceBMiller.com)

To invite Bruce to speak, contact him:

Website (BruceBMiller.com)

https://vimeo.com/159272951

Other Resources

The publishing ministry of Dadlin ministries—an organization committed to helping people develop wisdom for life.

Resources by **Bruce B. Miller**:

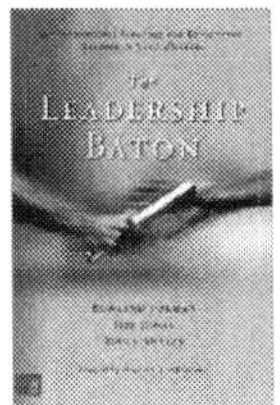

The Leadership Baton
Equips you with a solution to the need for quality leaders in local churches. Miller provides you with a biblical vision, a holistic approach and a comprehensive plan.

Your Life in Rhythm
Offers a realistic way to overcome our crazy, overly busy, stressed lives. Exposes the myth of living a "balanced" life. Miller presents "rhythmic living" as a new paradigm for relieving guilt and stress, so we can accomplish more of what matters most in life—with more freedom, peace, fulfillment and hope.

Your Church in Rhythm

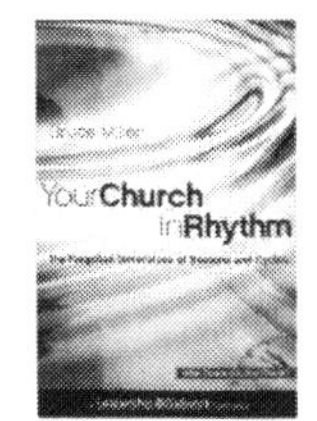

Most pastors try to do everything at once, and they feel guilty if even one aspect of their church ministry is neglected in the process. Instead, Miller proposes replacing this exhausting notion of "balance" with the true-to-life concept of "rhythm." Churches, just like people, should focus on the seasons and the cycles of ministry programs. That way, leaders can avoid burnout by focusing only on each issue at the time that it matters most.

Big God in a Chaotic World—A Fresh Look at Daniel
Shows we can live faithfully in this sinful, out-of-control world when we get a fresh vision of our big God. Daniel opens our eyes to see the God who is bigger than the problems in our world, bigger than all our fears, fires and lions.

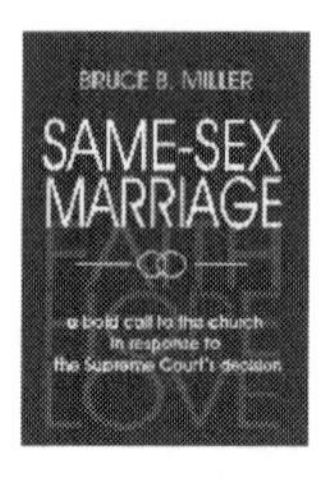

Same-Sex Marriage—A Bold Call to the Church in Response to the Supreme Court's Decision

In response to this cultural crisis, the church should step up with a Christlike response that stuns the world, and draws people to Jesus Christ with countercultural love.

Sexuality—Approaching Controversial Issues with Grace, Truth and Hope
Addresses the purposes of sex in marriage, singleness, cohabitation, homosexuality (and more), with fresh biblical insights filled with grace.

When God Makes No Sense—A Fresh Look at Habakkuk
By unpacking one chapter of Habakkuk at a time, Miller helps us see that when life is shaking you like a leaf in a storm, you can hold on to the unshakeable God who controls the storm.

Coming Soon:

Same-Sex Wedding—Should I Attend?
Miracles—A Fresh Look at Jesus

For more information on current and upcoming books, go to **BruceBMiller.com.**

McKinney, TX 75070

From the Author

Thank you for taking time to read this book. My hope is that you have found wisdom for your life. I love hearing from my readers. Feel free to contact me if you have any questions or thoughts you'd like to share. Email me at author@brucebmiller.com.

If you enjoyed this book, there are several things you can do to help others:

- Consider leaving a review on Amazon and on Goodreads, or your favorite online retailer. Honest reader reviews help others decide whether they'll enjoy a book.
- You can lend this book to a friend who might enjoy it.
- Check my website (BruceBmiller.com) or Facebook page (BruceBMillerAuthor) to find my other books and new releases. You can also sign up for my newsletter to receive the latest news.

Sincerely,

Bruce

Notes

1. Grant R. Osborne, *Exegetical Commentary on the New Testament: Matthew* (Grand Rapids: Zondervan, 2010), 165.

2. Max Lucado, *The Applause of Heaven—The Secret to a Truly Satisfying Life* (Nashville: Thomas Nelson, 1996).

3. William W. Klein, *Become What You Are: Spiritual Formation According to the Sermon on the Mount* (Tyrone, GA: Authentic Publishing, 2006), 75.

4. David L. Turner, *Matthew: Baker Exegetical Commentary on the New Testament* (Grand Rapids: Baker Academic, 2008), 76.

5. From "Hosanna" by Hillsong United.

6. (BAGD) [footnote the Greek lexicon]

7. Osborne, *Exegetical Commentary on the New Testament: Matthew*, 168.

8. Scot McKnight, *The Story of God Bible Commentary: Sermon on the Mount* (Grand Rapids: Zondervan, 2013), 47.

9. Klein, *Become What You Are*, 73.

10. Turner, *Matthew*, 83.

11. Klein, *Become What You Are*, 81.

12. (http://www.motherjones.com/politics/2013/04/domestic-violence-murder-stats)

13. (MARTIN LUTHER KING, JR., *Where Do We Go from Here: Chaos or Community?*, pp. 62–63 (1967) accessed at http://www.bartleby.com/73/1893.html)

14. (http://tipsofdivorce.com/tag/apps/)

15. N.T. Wright, *Matthew for Everyone*, Part 1, Chapters 1–15 (Louisville: Westminster John Knox Press, 2002), 49.

16. Haddon W. Robinson, *What Jesus Said about Successful Living: Principles from the Sermon on the Mount for Today* (Grand Rapids: Discovery House, 1991), 140.

17. McKnight, *The Story of God Bible Commentary: Sermon on the Mount*, 106.

18. Craig L. Blomberg, *The New American Commentary*: Volume 22, Matthew (Nashville: Broadman Press, 1992), 111.

19. Turner, *Matthew*, 50.

20. Klein, *Become What You Are*, 113.

21. D.A. Carson, *The Expositor's Bible Commentary: with the New International Version, Matthew*, Chapters 1-12 (Grand Rapids: Zondervan, 1984), 54.

22. John N. Day, *Truth Standing on Its Head: Insight for an Extraordinary Christian Walk from The Sermon on the Mount* (Nordskog: Venture, 2009), 81.

23. Osborne, *Exegetical Commentary on the New Testament: Matthew*, 232.

24. Osborne, *Exegetical Commentary on the New Testament: Matthew*, 237.

25. David Platt, *Christ-Centered Exposition: Exalting Jesus in Matthew* (Nashville: Holman Bible Publishers, 2013), 187.

26. (https://www.psychologytoday.com/articles/200007/waking-the-american-dream).

27. Klein, *Become What You Are*, 166.

28. Nicky Gumbel, *The Jesus Lifestyle* (Deerfield, IL: Alpha North America, 1993), 167.

29. Douglas Sean O'Donnell, *Matthew: All Authority in Heaven and on Earth* (Wheaton: Crossway, 2013), 177.

30. "I Know Who Holds Tomorrow", Songwriter Ira Stanphill. Lyrics © Capitol Christian Music Group.

31. Robinson, *What Jesus Said about Successful Living*, 236.

32. Gumbel. *The Jesus Lifestyle*, 183.

33. John R. W. Stott, *The Message of the Sermon on the Mount* (Matthew 5–7) (Downers Grove: InterVarsity Press, 1978), 178.

34. Robinson, *What Jesus Said about Successful Living,* 241.

35. Stott, *The Message of the Sermon on the Mount,* 179–180.

36. Robinson, *What Jesus Said about Successful Living,* 259. This has appeared in various versions with slightly different wording. Thought to be written by a Confederate Unknown Soldier.

37. John N. Day, *Truth Standing on Its Head,* 148.

63541194R00117

Made in the USA
Lexington, KY
11 May 2017